Surprised to be Standing:

A Spiritual Journey

by

Steven E. Brown, Ph.D.

A Healing Light Publication

"This is a compelling and thought provoking memoir. Steven Brown takes his reader on an intimate journey of discovery and re-discovery. Documenting a remarkable achievement of not only meeting a disability head on, but navigating his own pathway towards understanding how a life must be lived.
This is not just a book about perseverance amidst challenges-it is full of life altering-insight about the human condition and how hope propels us all."

Patricia Wood author of *Lottery*

"An initial encounter with Steve Brown's book suggests that is it an autobiographical memoir of a man with a disability. Yet, as the reader leafs through the textured life rendered on these pages, it becomes clear that these memoirs are not just the story of a life. Rather, the pages hold precious metaphors, poetry, and lessons for wayfinding. Metaphorically, Steve's life reflects to a large extent the movement of disability intellectual history, in which medical understandings of disability have been replaced with cultural, post modern and now productive and promising post-post modern explanations of this complex and unclear construct. The poetry contained in this volume is not only reflected in Steve's own formal poetic creations, but reveals itself to those who look for it in the way that his life emerged with rhythm and grace. And finally, wayfinding in this book is not simply navigation of the physical world, but rather being open to meet, shake hands with and move past painful obstacles in atypical ways.

Steve's life is a love story through which every reader can make meaning and follow this itinerary to healing, human relationships, and the contemplative life."

Elizabeth DePoy, Ph.D. and Stephen Gilson, Ph.D., University of Maine

"It's hard to imagine the agony Dr. Brown had to endure from the rare genetic disease he was diagnosed with as a small child and as he suffered from its worst symptoms throughout much of his life. This is a poignant and powerful autobiography of a man with Gaucher disease that shows us what a small boy can overcome and what he can accomplish as he grows into manhood. We all come across challenges in our lives and we choose, or our personal strength dictates, how we cope with those challenges. In his book *Surprised to be Standing: A Spiritual Journey,* Dr. Brown proves to us that he has both incredible inner strength and remarkable perseverance to overcome just about anything. Through Dr. Brown's suffering and spiritual awakenings and the founding of the Institute on Disability Culture, we learn of his amazing personal journey.

I take my hat off to Steven Brown and I applaud every painful bone in his body. Thank you for reminding us that through our own perseverance, we too can make a difference in our lives and others."

Cynthia J. Frank, Person with Gaucher disease, Director of Development for the National Gaucher Foundation

"Healing can be a fast process that sometimes does not require conscious participation of the one who seeks healing. It is my experience that it can require a long term commitment because a condition is a call for internal growth. This book is a prime example of the rewards one can ripen by following through with a commitment to participate in his own healing no matter what it might take."

Herwig Schoen, Founder of Reconnective Therapy

Surprised to be Standing: A Spiritual Journey

Published by Healing Light:
http://www.healinglighthawaii.org

Library of Congress Control Number: 2011900964

Brown, Steven E.
Surprised to be standing: A spiritual journey/ by Steven E. Brown

ISBN-13: 978-1456521691
ISBN-10:1456521691

Other Publications by Steven E. Brown
(More information at: http://www.instituteondisabilityculture.org)

Movie Stars and Sensuous Scars:
Essays on the Journey from Disability Shame to Disability Pride

Poetry

Dragonflies In Paradise: An Activist's Partial Poetic Autobiography

The Goddess Approaches Fifty: Poems

Journey Home:
A Miracles Poetry, Prayer, And Meditation Workbook

Love into Forever:
A Tribute to Martyrs, Heroes, Friends, and Colleagues

Pain, Plain--And Fancy Rappings:
Poetry From The Disability Culture

Voyages--Life Journeys

Monographs

A Celebration of Diversity:
An Annotated Bibliography about Disability Culture, 2nd Ed.

Celebrating Passion, Relentlessness, And Vision: The Manifesto Editorials

Independent Living: Theory & Practice

Investigating A Culture Of Disability: Final Report

For Younger Readers:

Ed Roberts: Wheelchair Genius

This book is dedicated to

all who serve as mentors,

guides, and role models,

old and young,

visible and invisible;

to generations in my own life-

past, present, and future;

and to

spiritual journeys.

Table of Contents

Acknowledgements

While writing is often a solitary task, moving words from the mind to the world is not. Many individuals shared a part in the evolution of this book from manuscript to publication. I am grateful to each one, sometimes more than I can possibly put into words, but words I can share.

Without my parents and their support, nothing I have written about in these pages would have happened and I am happy both my Mom and Dad lived long enough to see the changes described herein. I don't always paint my family in the best light--like any family we have differences, personality clashes, and distinct ways of viewing the world. But my family is a fundamentally supportive one, always willing to lend a hand, offer a kind word, and be present when it counts. These traits may not always come across in the tales told in this book, but I will be forever grateful for each member of my family.

My wife, Lillian Gonzales Brown, is my staunchest supporter and advocate. She listened to every word of at least one version of the manuscript and made critically important comments, as did the following readers, who commented on various stages of the work: Nancy Aleck, Charmaine Crockett, Elizabeth DePoy, Cyndi Frank, Stephen Gilson, Aimée Gramblin, Alice Griffin, Helen Kutz, Mark Medoff, Sharie Phillips-Swatek, Herwig Schoen, Kerstin Schoen, and Patricia Wood.

A special thank you to instructors Anne D. LeClaire, Dan Millman, and my fellow students in two Hawai'i Writer's Retreats. Together the first few pages of this book have been massaged many times. More importantly, the Retreats led to supportive, critical, and empathetic friendships and colleagues. Most importantly, being around others who wondered what I wrote about, rather than what I did, refreshed and re-energized me. Thanks to Dan for subtitle suggestions. I finally found one I liked! Thanks to Anne for her always gracious support.

My daughter, Aimée Gramblin, a fellow writer, has been incredibly patient and supportive of her Dad's penchant to write about his perspectives and feelings about her over the years and I'm grateful she continues to be willing to be portrayed in print.

I first met the exuberant novelist Patricia Wood as a student. We have both delighted in our changing roles, as we've become friends and mutual mentors. Pat has been a delight in sharing her own stories of writing and publishing.

Herwig Schoen has been a friend, mentor, and healer in my life since the day we met. Meeting him literally changed my life for the better as described within these pages. Without our friendship this particular book would never have been written--because my story would be a different one.

In the course of writing autobiographical memories, it is sometimes painfully obvious whose viewpoint is being shared-- mine, naturally. I am especially grateful to everyone who supports my autobiographical writing habit with love and to everyone else who puts up with it.

I have done my best to ensure these memories are both as accurate and as true to my own feelings as possible. But mistakes are likely to have been made and I accept full responsibility for any errors. In some cases, names have been changed if permission has not been requested or granted to use someone's true identity.

Finally, this is my story. My hope is it will resonate with others, but I make no claim anyone else would share the same experiences I did—it remains, after all, my story.

Note: Reconnective Therapy (RCT) is not a medical treatment and is not intended to replace appropriate medical practice. For more information on RCT, see: http://www.reconnectivetherapy.com

Photo credits: Cover photo of Steven E. Brown and back cover photo by Trip Rems, *http://www.auroragalleries.com*
AUCD, 2008, by Robert C. Johnson.
All other photographs, photographer unknown.

Part I: Pain

Every time I manage to stand,

I am extremely grateful,

especially since it hurts as much

to be sitting as it does to stand.

December 19, 1968

Chapter 1:

"A Walking Miracle"

Character cannot be developed in ease and quiet.
Only through experience of trial and suffering can
the soul be strengthened, vision cleared, ambition
inspired, and success achieved.

Helen Keller

I wanted to scream. Soft, whimpering sounds of pain didn't satisfy. I needed to howl, cry, screech. I lay awake in the middle of the night in my brother's bedroom, the one with the shared bathroom. He slept in my remodeled basement room in Portage, Michigan, a semi-rural township next to the small southwestern city of Kalamazoo. My parents and sister occupied the two other bedrooms on this level of the house. I used my brother's bed when sick because I couldn't climb the basement steps. I couldn't do much of anything.

I wanted to scream. No other outlets for my frustration existed. The pain consumed me, permeating every aspect of my being, drawing each second into hours. Nights dragged on into eternity. When the neighborhood quieted, all the lights turned off, I heard only crickets and other nocturnal nature sounds. I lay wide awake, immersed in my hurting body. I tried to read but put the book down. Screaming softly when I wanted to shout to the night skies as loudly as possible demanding why me, why do I suffer?

In my early teens, in the mid-1960s, resenting my body, my

pain, my disease, my life, I cursed God. I couldn't understand why I'd been saddled with my burden, most visible in many episodes of excruciating immobility.

Once, as a senior in high school, in the midst of what's now known as "bone crises," but which we then called "attacks," persistent, agonizing, excruciating joint pain—cause unknown—I counted the minutes to move. The effort, the determination, the perseverance to go from laying to sitting to standing to moving. This activity, so simple most people complete it in seconds, lasted more than thirty minutes. Years later I described it poetically:

I lie. I decide to get up. To go to the bath-room. To go to bed. To get something to eat. To see another room. To do something. I decide to get up.

Not I get up. This is conscious, deliberate. It will happen no other way.

I decide to get up.

I move. I scream. I hurt. Maybe I won't get up.

*I **decide** to get up.*

I move.

I scream. I hurt. I will get up. I will get up. I move.

My body begins to move with me. All of it. Except the knee.

Slowly, deliberately, painstakingly, I lift my

knee.

I drag it to a sitting position.

I exhale.

I rest.

I sweat.

I'm exhausted.

I hurt.

I curse.

I breathe.

I decide to stand.

I move. I scream. I hurt. Maybe I won't stand.

*I **decide** to stand.*

I move.

I scream. I hurt. I will stand. I will stand.

I move.

My body begins to move with me. All of it.

Except the knee.

Slowly, deliberately, tenderly, I lift my knee.

I drag it to a standing position.

I exhale.

I rest.

I sweat.

I'm exhausted.

I hurt.

Curse.

Breathe.

Decide to move.

I move. I scream. I hurt. Maybe I won't
move.

*I **decide** to move.*

I move.

I scream. I hurt. I will move. I will move.

I move.

My body begins to move with me. All of it.

Except the knee.

Slowly, deliberately, tenderly, consciously,
painstakingly, I lift my knee. I drag it alongside
me as I move.

I exhale.

I rest.

I sweat.

Exhausted, I arrive.

Hurting.

Cursing.

Breathing.

I await the next time I need to move.

I can wait for a long time, I think.

But, of course, I cannot.

When I wrote this poem, in my early forties, I
could only imagine the rest of my life immersed in pain
and immobility. Ten years later my life had changed. A

frightening medical test in my late forties compelled me to choose between ongoing pain and desperation or healing and liberation. After a fifty-year struggle, I am "a walking miracle."

Chapter 2:

Mystery Limp

The physical examination disclosed a
well developed, well nourished alert
and cooperative boy in no distress.
S. B. Hayles [M.D.], Mayo Clinic, October 1, 1957

Imagine a five year-old boy playing on an autumn evening in 1957, on the freshly paved streets of a newly constructed neighborhood. My sixth birthday approaches in late October. I'm one of the youngest kids in my first grade class. It's time to return home for the evening and I'm limping, but I don't know why.

I don't remember this limp. Fragments of recollection survive: my Mom telling me I complained my right leg hurt; a memory of my Dad standing in front of our hall closet, probably getting out or putting away a jacket, not knowing what else to do; or my parents seeing their eldest son, who loved running around outside, limping. Doctors in Kalamazoo couldn't diagnose the cause of the limp. My parents finally chose to take me to the Mayo Clinic in Rochester, Minnesota, where my Dad's parents, who lived in Kalamazoo, traveled for treatment of their own medical ailments.

Weeks shy of my sixth birthday I climbed steep airplane steps for the first time, squealing with delight to board with my Mom and grandmother, anticipating adventure. Mom dealt with the two of us and the onset of her third pregnancy. My father stayed home with

Marty, born two and a half years after me, and whom I generally considered my bratty younger brother. I hoped, maybe more desperately than my parents, for a sister.

Tidbits from my time in the Clinic remain. A sprawling building with brown walls and light floors. Symbols that, I believe, guided us to our destination. Beyond the shadows of the walls, little memory lingers—but scars remain. Lines, a quarter-inch wide, dissect my outer thighs. My right leg bears the longer mark, eight inches down, but the biopsy of my left leg revealed my fate: Gaucher's (pronounced Go-shays) Disease.

In 1882, Philippe Gaucher, a French medical student, identified this recessive, genetic disorder. Gaucher Disease, known in the 1950s, when I was diagnosed, as Gaucher's Disease (GD), is a recessive, genetic disorder, originally believed to be most common among individuals, like me, with an Ashkenazic (usually Eastern European) Jewish familial history, but now identified in numerous ethnic groups.

GD is metabolic in origin, resulting in lowered production of an enzyme called glucocerebrosidase intended to discharge a fatty substance, or lipid, called glucocerebroside. GD blocks the elimination of glucocerebroside so it remains in the body, sometimes wreaking havoc, as detailed in following chapters.

Three general types of GD have been recognized. I was born with Type 1, commonly referred to as the adult type, meaning we are anticipated to have an average lifespan, unlike those with Types 2 and 3, who still die at an early age, during infancy or adolescence.

Type 1 GD can lead to a build-up of glucocerebroside in

bones and in organs, such as the spleen and liver. These accumulations are generically labeled Gaucher cells.

Where the GD cells concentrate they tend to cause sometimes significant problems because of interference with typical production of, for example, platelets or bone regeneration. In some cases, as with me, GD symptoms can be extremely painful, leading to broken bones and the secondary condition of arthritis or excruciating bone crises, resulting from a lack of oxygen or blood supply to joints or bones.

Many of these details were unknown in my childhood, when GD first manifested. Even the name has changed. We used the plural form, Gaucher's, during my childhood. Today, the accepted form is Gaucher Disease. In both cases the abbreviation GD applies. In this story the plural or singular form is used to match the time described. In 1957, doctors understood GD as a progressive, genetic disease frequently resulting in bone pain and liver and spleen distress. No one knew the cause the disease. At the post-biopsy conference, my mother listened to the pieces of knowledge physicians then possessed.

Any child who inherits a combination of the recessive and dominant gene for GD, as my sister did, becomes a carrier of the disease, but doesn't experience symptoms. A child with two dominant genes, like my brother, neither experiences symptoms nor passes the disease forward to his descendants. Inheriting the recessive GD genes from both parents, I had the disease.

Reporting to my hometown doctor, on October 11, 1957, the Mayo Clinic's Dr. Hayles wrote:

Dear Dr. Margolis. Thank you very much for your confidence in asking us to see your patient. I am sure you remember his history and I will not review it at this time. He was admitted to the Clinic on October 1...complaining of migratory joint and leg pains.

With these findings the patient was seen in consultation by a member of the section on orthopedic surgery. Bone biopsy was recommended. The boy was hospitalized...bone marrow biopsy was obtained from both the right and left femur. Microscopic examination of the tissue removed from the right disclosed only evidence of necrosis and clusters of fatty acid crystals. The material from the left contained numerous Gaucher's cells.

We discussed Gaucher's disease at length with Mrs. Brown and I believe that she has accepted these findings as well as one could expect.

It is our feeling that this disease will be slowly progressive, but that it is anticipated the boy should have no significant difficulty for many years.

Home from Rochester, eager to resume my first grade life, we played football in the front yard of my friend Andy's house, which stood at one end of our block. My cropped hair, dark brown like the rest of my family—except for what remained of Dad's once iron curls, graying at the temples—bristled in the fall air. Holding the ball and running toward our makeshift goal, someone tackled me. I fell. I tried to get up, but couldn't. My leg wouldn't budge. Andy ran inside yelling for help.

The femur in my right leg, full of necrotic GD cells and weakened from the recent biopsy, snapped. No one anticipated this. I spent my sixth birthday in the hospital.

My fractured leg healed and I didn't break any more bones until adolescence. But my disease changed my life. Each spring and fall, as the Michigan seasons turned, so did my body.

A knee swelled to the size of a softball. Shrieking when trying to walk, my parents carried me. But the jarring of their steps, out of my control, made me want to scream more than my own crawling. I began to fear another's touch, unable to distinguish between a doctor's heavy hands palpitating my tender joints or a feathery stroke of love.

Bone infarctions—that's what they call the swelling now. Our word, "attacks," better captures my experience. The pain seared every corner of my soul.

A pang. A funny feeling. A sense. Somehow I knew: my time had come. My mother knew it too. We kept it secret. Why worry anyone else? It might not come. But it always did.

A day. Maybe two or three. I'd feel it in my knee. Then something grew, inflated. I could barely see it, but I knew my knee swelled. Pain twinged—barely tangible. But I knew it would spread until the day I couldn't get up, couldn't move, could deny the pain no longer.

I'd want to be alone. Who wanted to inflict this pain on anyone else? My family tiptoed around me. I didn't want to move. I didn't want to breathe.

At its worst, I could barely tolerate food. I chewed nuts. Nothing else. We learned the hard way. I tried other things, but nothing else stayed down. Nuts: cashews have a lovely curve-- tender, undulating. Walnuts are like a saw, striated, just enough space for the tongue to lap the salt. Almonds are best whole, unless split exactly in half. Hazel nuts are hard, yet easy; whole, yet small. Did nuts feel pain when the nutcracker pierced their tough shells? Brazil nuts are odd—sometimes the flaxy taste one wants; other times, a waxy flavor to avoid. Peanuts, last eaten, filled about half the mixed nuts can. Eating nuts provided momentary diversion—an entertaining few seconds. I didn't know why my body tolerated only nuts. I still don't.

The beginning of the end appeared with another subtle sensation. My Mom sensed it too. One sign: a hankering for a Hershey cake my Mom made. When I asked for this dessert everyone knew. The end dawned. The cake marked celebration, relief.

Bone crises lasted about two weeks. The memories linger a lifetime.

Chapter 3:

Alone

July 27, 1966

Dear Mrs. Brown:

I am not sure I understand your request for me to "give any advice on what to do concerning the bone growth problem." It is somewhat puzzling to learn Steve is still having discomfort in the same area of the left leg which was involved in an acute pain episode in May. This does suggest a careful review since one does not expect continuing troubles after these bouts.

With best regards,

Allen C. Crocker [M.D.]

I made straight "A's" until fifth or sixth grade. In junior high school, seventh through ninth grade, "C's" and "B's became a struggle. My teachers and parents scolded me. "How do you expect to get into college if you can't do better than this?" My life, my pain, interfered with the goals others hoped for me. But I didn't know how to articulate such thoughts. I didn't know what I thought. I lived in pain, physical and psychic. I concentrated on putting one foot forward.

Our annual summer vacations gave me a break from these stresses. The summer before eighth grade, Jimmy Fund Children's Charity billboards loomed ahead as we traversed Boston's Brookline

Avenue toward Children's Hospital. My parents had learned about Dr. Allen Crocker, a renowned physician working in the area of pediatrics and developmental disabilities. We'd arranged our annual summer vacation trip around a visit to his office.

Dr. Crocker gently measured and poked. He pronounced a gap almost an inch long between the lengths of my legs. He speculated my longer right leg resulted from my football fracture. I'd require special shoes, or a lift placed on the bottom of my shoe's left heel, to compensate for the three-quarter inch difference. Needing to wear shoes all the time to prevent back pain, I still miss the feeling of tendrils of grass beneath my bare feet.

In my fourteenth summer I noticed persistent, sometimes breath-taking twinges of pain, like a serrated knife slicing along the inside of my left hip, near my groin. My physician ordered X-rays, which in the 1960s could be more painful than any ache.

Tall, long metal tables lay underneath enormous X-ray machines whose length often matched that of half to three-quarters of the table. The machine's width was about the same dimension as the table and maybe half as deep. To have pictures taken by this elaborate apparatus, we wore wafer-thin gowns rarely covering our entire bodies, always exposing at least a portion of our behinds.

Climbing onto the table, with my aching hip, would be unpleasant, but worse awaited—a frigid metal tabletop. I dreaded the next step when the X-ray technician brusquely positioned my body at the best angles for picture-taking, disregarding my aching body. Whatever hurt when entering an X-ray room worsened during the process.

Once the technician found the optimum pose I'd be commanded to hold still. The technician moved to a nearby alcove to operate the machine. Through a microphone I'd hear the instruction, "Don't breathe." I'd play statue while the machine whirred. With the single word "Breathe," I'd relax. The process recurred until finishing all the X-rays the doctor ordered.

Helping me off the table, the technician directed us to wait while the film processed. The pictures needed to be of sufficient quality to please the doctor. It frequently took an hour or longer to develop these films. I'd try to read but the lingering pain from the process I'd just undergone and my own impatience led concentration to elude me. I waited in fear. The entire process had to be repeated if the X-rays didn't show the needed angle or proper clarity.

The doctor delivered his verdict. He couldn't detect the origin of the pain.

None of us gave up because the pain continued. In the fall, another X-ray revealed a healing, hairline hip fracture. I used crutches to keep weight off my recovering left hip.

My doctor admonished me that my broken hip signaled a need to be cautious with my body. No more running or jumping. Sports were out of the question. I swallowed hard. Tears may have welled. But it was fall in Michigan; I could live without sports, without running or jumping while the temperatures froze and the snow fell.

My best friend Craig lived next door. We'd meet in our basements. The same words often came out of our mouths at the same time. "1-2-3 you owe me a Coke." Our mantra when this happened. We became interested in psychic phenomena which we called ESP, extra-sensory perception. I picked up books about such experiences. Reading in winter increased since I couldn't play in the snow anymore.

When spring poked through the winter haze a few months later I couldn't help myself. I wanted to take advantage. In the past year or so my gangliness began to evolve into coordination. I'd felt athletic in my body as well as my desires and hoped to try out for the school baseball team. No one forgot my physician's warning, but I couldn't remain still while the birds began to sing and flowers to bloom. I could taste the dust of an athletic field. I knew I'd find my friends on our nearby baseball diamonds. I grabbed my mitt.

I didn't slink out of the house. I discussed my desire to test the doctor's conclusion with my parents. "Did I have to do this? Didn't I think the doctor knew what he was talking about?' It didn't matter. The physician had been clear: I "could never again jump or run without risking further injury." But I couldn't help it. I had to test my body, to know it could endure. "Okay, do what you have to do."

I walked outside to join my friends. We tossed the ball to one another in the field and practiced our swings. I strolled to the plate holding the bat over my right shoulder. I dug in, staring at the pitcher who glared back at me. He released the ball and I swung, my first hit of the season. Within seconds of running to first base I knew my hip fractured. Dismayed and scared I told no one. My life just changed forever and I blocked this reality to enjoy one last day of athletic freedom.

I limped home. My mother glanced at me, then dialed the phone to make a doctor's appointment. Somehow she refrained from saying "I told you so." My doctor calmly informed me if I attempted such foolishness again I'd likely require surgery, a hospital stay, and bone grafts from one part of my body to another. He meant to scare me and he succeeded.

Walking on crutches once more, my dreams of athletic prowess evaporated, but not my love affair with sports. Perhaps I could be a sports journalist. I contacted the local Portage weekly newspaper and I started a sports opinion column called "Brown's Beat."

External 1960s events impacted me as strongly as my internal tensions. I watched the civil rights movement unfold. Charismatic leader Martin Luther King, Jr. snared the nation's attention when at a 1963 March on Washington he told us he had a dream:

> *I have a dream that my four little children will one day live in a nation where they will not be judged by the color of their skin, but by the content of their character....And when this happens, and when we allow freedom to ring—when we let it ring from every village and every hamlet, from every state and every city, we will be able to speed up that day when all of God's children—black men and white men, Jews and Gentiles, Protestants and Catholics—will be able to join hands and sing in the words of the old Negro spiritual: Free at last, free at last, thank God Almighty, we are free at last!*

King became one of my heroes. An early protester of the Vietnam War, he recognized the toll it took on black Americans. He also battled the capitalist system that ghettoized his people. In Memphis, in March 1968, King lent his support to striking black garbage workers. A month later he returned to that city and in a speech called "I've Been to the Mountaintop" he relayed he'd made it to the top of the mountain and peered over it to view a new dawn, a new life of freedom for black—and white—Americans. He also wondered if he'd live to see his dream become reality in part because he received numerous death threats. This wasn't idle speculation. Standing on the balcony of his Memphis hotel, an assassin fatally shot him.

Stunned, I watched the TV news reports about King's death, then walked to my bedroom, shut the door, pulled out a notebook and began writing. I reflected on King's death and how I wanted to change the world. I wanted to live on a planet where all people were treated with equality and justice. I hoped to become an impactful writer.

The turmoil of the late 1960s matched my own internal strife. Home life—supportive in so many ways throughout bone crises and bone breaks, learning to drive, participating in social activities, traveling—became increasingly stifling at fifteen, sixteen, seventeen. My brother, sister and I engaged in questioning and spirited conversations at the family dinner table, encouraged by our parents. But when I explored doubts about deeply held religious and social beliefs, our family ritual became oppressive. I wanted to probe issues of interest, including politics and religion. But I so outraged my father he quashed all conversation. One day I simply chose to keep my mouth shut. With each passing day I repeated a mantra: I'd leave home in three years; two years; one year; six months. Until then I'd guard my thoughts. I retreated to my bedroom, my haven of privacy.

Chapter 4:

Diary

When seen on November 21, 1968, the patient was having distress and disability of the left hip and left knee. The patient walked with a definite antalgic gait on the left. There was considerable tenderness elicited over the left greater trochanter, but no tenderness or effusion of the left knee was noted. All motions of the left hip were limited. In December of 1968, the patient had another flare-up of Gaucher's disease which lasted for about two weeks.

Robert J. Graham, M.D., Sept. 23, 1969
Practice Limited to Orthopedic Surgery

In the summer of 1968, before my senior year in high school, my Dad accepted a better paying job in another state. We moved into a small rental home in East Moline, Illinois. One of several northwestern Illinois locales on the banks of the Mississippi River, known as the Quad Cities, East Moline sat adjacent to Moline and across the magnificent Mississippi from Davenport, Iowa. On the other side of Moline lay Rock Island, the largest of the Illinois cities.

While Dad acclimated to his new State Hospital job, my brother and I learned about our new high school, United Township. It served lots of smaller, surrounding communities and totaled about 4,000 students. One building couldn't accommodate us all, so freshmen and sophomores used the old high school while juniors and seniors attended the newer one. Marty rode a bus to his school, while I'd walk, bus, or drive. Once or twice a year, the entire school gathered in one building for an assembly, displaying the area's diversity—middle class kids, redneck families, farmers, city boys and girls, Mexicans (not yet called Chicanos or Latinos or Hispanics), blacks, and a variety of religions, dominated by fundamentalist Christians.

I joined the debate team and Junior Achievement, a vocational club where I focused on radio and television. These extra-curricular activities kept me busy during my senior year.

My brother and I shared a small room, sleeping in bunk beds. For a modicum of privacy, I carved out a small space in the basement and covered the wall above a desk with sports articles and memorabilia of other passions.

We also found a new orthopedist, Dr. Graham, reputed to be the area's best. A bear of a man, sporting a waxed, handlebar mustache, Dr. Graham loved his job. He spent the first part of each day in surgery, seeing patients in the late afternoon and evening. Rather than going in at my scheduled appointment time, we'd call to see how much later we should arrive. We spent three hours with Dr. Graham during our first meeting. Impatient waiting room faces stared at us when we walked out of his office, but Dr. Graham believed in taking his time and being thorough. Being scheduled for 4 p.m. might mean getting in to see him at 7 or 8 in the evening.

As in Michigan, my body changed with the seasons. Western Illinois had a somewhat gentler climate than southwestern Michigan and I responded a little later in the year to the change. With my focus now on writing, I decided to keep a diary during a bone crisis. Two entries follow:

12/19/68

I didn't get much sleep last night. I woke up at 2:30 A.M. and moved from my bed to the couch. I have been there since, always with a heating pad on my hip. Needless to say I was absent from school today.

Indeed today I have been bothered by so much pain that I pray [it] does not increase. In addition to the constant dull pain in my hip joint, is the sharp pain that pierces my nerve center when I attempt to move my limb.

It is a major effort to go from a laying down position to sitting up and much more painful to try to stand. When I want to sit I gently maneuver my leg from the couch onto the floor, with the rest of my body following. This is relatively simple and painless when compared to trying to stand.

It is unbearable to put weight on my right leg, so I am using crutches. I take my crutches in my right hand and push with my left hand and leg. This sounds easy, but it's not. Usually when I have just managed to leave the couch, piercing pain runs through my joint. Every time I manage to stand, I am extremely grateful, especially since it hurts as much to be sitting as it does to stand.

With the unrelentess [sic] pain I am taking a steady

dose of medication, but it does little or no good. I ran out of codeine pills, which were much more effective than all my other medicine, so for the latter part of the day the pain has been gradually worsening.

While I was home today I viewed TV and read. I didn't think I read enough last time I was sick, so today I read the Sporting News, finished a Time (from 2 weeks ago) and read The Wisdom of Martin Luther King. The last time I was sick all I read in addition to the Sporting News and Time were Oedipus Rex, Macbeth, the last half of King Lear and the first half of The Making of a President: 1960.

My diet has consisted of an apple, two glasses of milk, half a sandwich, some fish, salad and corn and a can of pop. I was pushed into eating so much.

Today, I remembered I should have realized an attack was coming, because for the past week and a half it has been almost impossible for me to stay seated longer than half an hour.

Tonight we celebrated the fourth night of Hanukah, which I enjoyed little. I doubt that my Christmas vacation will be spectacular either. That reminds me that tonight I was supposed to play Santa Claus in our Junior Achievement TV company's Christmas special. I was looking forward to it and am disappointed someone else had to be chosen.

Today only one thing has annoyed me tremendously besides the pain and that is noise. The more noise I hear the more irritable I get, which makes life miserable for everyone else.

Now, some more pain-killers and off to sleep—I hope.
1/4/68 [sic-should be 69]
No pain.

Later that year, enraged over some slight, beyond flustered and lacking control over my life, I descended the basement stairs, in more of a frenzy with each step, and ripped everything I'd lovingly created and placed on the walls into shreds. My Mom yelled, "Why can't you act like everyone else?" I shouted, "I'm not like everyone else!" I stormed into our bedroom, lay on the bottom bunk and tried to calm myself. Maybe an hour later Dad knocked. He sat at the edge of the bed, and let me know Mom regretted our exchange. This conversation for the first time acknowledged the emotion of how I differed from everyone else and got me through the next few days.

During the latter part of my senior high school year, I started experiencing severe pains in my left hip, the one I'd previously fractured. Dr. Graham recommended I strap on a full-length hip brace to alleviate weight and pressure on my hip.

Two metal bars along the length of the brace fortified a plastic cup supporting my hip. My left shoe screwed into the brace so it became a one-piece contraption, from shoe to hip. In cold weather, the metal sent icy sensations down my skin. Screws at each side of my knee held in place a bar I'd maneuver to bend the apparatus to be able to sit. At all times, I walked with a straight gait. The bar around the brace at my knee widened my pants leg so everyone could observe something different about me.

At the end of my senior high school year in East Moline, re-signed to my strange way of walking, I headed for college at South-ern Illinois University in Carbondale, as far south and warm as I could travel and retain in-state tuition.

Chapter 5:

Caves, Tear Gas, and Revolution

I am delighted to hear that Steven is getting
along well and that he has learned to accommodate to
his disease. Enclosed you will find a copy of the letter
we wrote at the time of Steven's dismissal from the
Clinic. This letter should be transmitted to the draft
board. I feel confident that Steven will not be a candi-
date for military service.
S. B. Hayles, M.D., July 8, 1970

Carbondale epitomized a college town. Strip mining de-
pleted the area's coal and Southern Illinois University (SIU) became
the town's big business. Twenty thousand SIU students supported
professors, other university personnel, and merchants, in a town of
40,000.

In my first days on campus I met Bobby and Scott, who became my closest friends. Both graduated from junior colleges and
traveled "west" from east coast cities. We sat together for many
meals. While I slowly consumed heaps of food we'd discuss politics,
money, and women. My still growing, gangly frame had lots of room
to pack in the chow. In high school, I'd dreamed of becoming 6'2."
As a college freshman I shot two inches past that to my full height of
6'4."

I'd planned to be at SIU for two years, then transfer to a

school in the west, where my body would appreciate warmer weather. SIU's flexible General Studies curriculum, which gave two years to declare a major, meant I could sample various fields. I intended to immerse myself in the college's many offerings, both in classes and out in the world.

Rebellion permeated our lives. Our history professor declared he wouldn't penalize students who boycotted class to protest the Vietnam War during a National Moratorium Day. I participated and contributed to SIU's reputation as Illinois' most radical college campus. But my political bent soon gave way to the charms of a dorm resident I met at the beginning of SIU's 2nd quarter.

Quince didn't ridicule me when I mentioned my feelings about extra-sensory perception. "What could I do?" I told him about moments I perceived someone wanting to contact me and it'd happen, or time spent communicating with various friends, but hardly speaking a word. Quince said he'd experienced telepathy, astral projection, and precognition. "Would I like to meet three of his friends? They spent most days exploring their minds." I became an eager disciple.

Bobby and Scott wondered why I stopped eating with them, but I wouldn't, couldn't, share and they quickly decided to ignore me. I didn't care.

Quince and his friends—Dixie, Brad, and Annie—tentatively let me into their circle. We'd burn candles and peer through the light into one another's auras and infinitely malleable shapes. Quince's transformation burned into my consciousness. Dark and intense, the lines of his body dissipated into wavy colors. Red. Green. White.

Black. His huge head dominated my internal sight. He smiled as he invaded my soul. How did he work his way into me? I didn't know, but sensing his presence within frightened me. Wanting him gone, I withdrew from this exercise.

On one occasion, we meditated in a quiet Student Union space and our minds melded almost into one. We explored the low, rough, brown ceiling and narrow, craggy halls of a cave. All of us were there, but I was alone, prone, apart from the rest of them. I wanted to rise but feared the consequences to my flimsy skull. I lay still, fearful. Jeans tattered, shirt dripping with sweat. Somewhere nearby I discerned voices and a light. A dull yellow almost reached me. Low voices, excited murmurs taunted. Perhaps I could join the group whose voices wended their way to me. Projecting my internal voice as loudly as possible, desperate to be heard, only silence reverberated. I stretched, closed my eyes and listened. Straining, tensing, trying to see them, only whispers reached me.

Feet glided over steps. Voices faded. The group vanished. I heard faint murmurs. They couldn't be far. If only I could narrow the distance. I strained and concentrated, but only my mind grasped their presence. The four of them explored the cave and each other, while I remained behind. When we awoke from our trance I knew I could never maintain their pace, but there was so much to learn I wanted to stay.

Quince wanted me around too, less for my mind than my body. I lacked interest, but cherished Quince's companionship. One day, about a month after meeting, we sat in his dorm room, both knowing what he wanted. Wearing me down, we undressed and his mouth engulfed me. New to someone else's lips on my intimate parts, I lay back thinking perhaps I could enjoy this. I relaxed a bit, but not enough. Quince didn't realize how naive I was. I flinched when he thrust his manhood at me but he pressed. Reluctantly, I placed my mouth over his rod. I blanched, tried again. I couldn't do it. I quit. I had no conception how devastating rejection would be. I didn't realize the depth of my naivety. The magic vanished. Quince didn't trust anyone he couldn't manipulate. Despite my ugly encounter with his flesh I still wanted to learn from him, to communicate telepathically, to join the group in the cave or wherever else they might go. I wished to enhance my parapsychological powers.

I persisted, as did Quince. He focused his charm and power. Lying alone in my dorm room I felt his presence—cajoling, manipulating. Being attacked by someone not in my physical presence terrified me. If he could penetrate my consciousness in this way what else might he do? Fighting his advances, I think I defied his aggression only because in my great innocence I failed to understand the power of so sensual a being.

I began noticing unappealing group dynamics. I watched Dixie sensually manipulate Quince, Brad and Annie. We never trusted one another so within the group she openly despised me. I didn't much like being around her and avoided her when I could.

I began to see in this quartet a definition of evil, a word I didn't use lightly. They cared so little about other people nothing stopped them from seeking their own gratification. I chose to remove myself from them as far as I could. Not only physically, but in every other way. I feared them and what they might do to me. I didn't possess the power to protect myself from their psychic assaults, so I chose to block that part of my life, believing I selected good over evil. When I sought Bobby and Scott again, they shook their heads at me expressing a few moments of confusion at my months of disappearance, then welcomed me back. While I'd focused on myself, they'd concentrated on their studies. Unlike me, they'd be drafted into the military if they left college for any reason. Then in the spring of 1970, all other endeavors, extracurricular or not, succumbed to the dominance of our undeclared war in Vietnam. President Nixon, despised by many, but elected at least in part because of his 1968 campaign promise to end this war, made a startling announcement: the United States sponsored an incursion into Vietnam's neighbor, Cambodia, to eliminate enemy sanctuaries.

The invasion of Cambodia lit an inextinguishable fire. Peace activists arose in record numbers, resulting in the largest campus protests in the nation's history. Over a million students and half of America's twenty-five hundred college campuses witnessed protests. Peaceful demonstrations drew adequate crowds until we learned the National Guard gunned down four students at Kent State in nearby Ohio. The governor of Ohio requested the National Guard's presence at Kent State in what we perceived as overreaction to protests there. Standing on the steps of the University's Administration Building, young and inexperienced members of the Guard panicked. First names, then rocks and bottles had been tossed at them. Scared, they fired and four students paid the price with their lives. What would happen now on other college campuses? What could we do to display our support for the slain students, immediate martyrs?

Furious that the government expanded the fight from Southeast Asia to American college campuses where American students had become the enemy, too, we wouldn't submit. We'd protest. Bobby and Scott demonstrated that night, while I chose to focus on my studies after my dalliance with Quince and his gang. About nine or ten o'clock I heard angry voices. A couple hundred students had protested the war and the Kent State murders. Cops arrived and name-calling ensued. The police, disparagingly called "pigs," didn't sit by idly. They attacked. Bobby's roommate displayed the bruise on his head where a club struck him. Bobby and Scott showered us with narratives of police brutality and narrow escapes.

How dare anyone treat my friends with violence and disrespect? The three warriors said another demonstration would occur the next evening. Would I join them? I had no intention of missing it.

Talk around campus the next day centered on the demonstration and violence of the night before and the action planned for today. So many people wanted to be involved in the night's protest, preparatory meetings were called.

Bobby, Scott, and I walked toward the common area for the preliminary meetings and the starting point of the march. Speakers climbed onto a platform. We'd shown up to share our support for ending the war. We'd march to demonstrate solidarity with those who lost their lives at Kent State. We'd calmly arise as one in a few minutes and march a mile from the middle of campus to downtown Carbondale. We'd hold high our signs and sing songs of peace and freedom proclaiming our desire for the war's end.

We'd all seen the National Guard. Passing the campus Armory on our way to the meeting we observed Guardsmen standing outside and preparing tanks for action. Illinois' Governor, like his Ohio counterpart, had called for reinforcements.

Campus leaders warned us to bring jackets and handkerchiefs in case the Guard used tear gas. If that happened we knew to calmly cover our faces and breathe into our protective cloths.

At least a thousand strong we marched the mile to downtown. We avoided the Armory, but couldn't help passing some Guardsmen. A few cries of "pigs" and "murderers" split the air, but most of us remained silent, communing with ourselves. A few Guardsmen retaliated with insults of cowardice and betrayal. Most stayed quiet.

Bobby, Scott, and I walked solemnly, excitedly, experiencing frequent mood swings. Downtown, merchants stared at us. No prior training prepared them for this experience. Business owners guarded their front doors, concerned about vandalism and looting. Some sympathized with the protestors, some vilified us, but most feared our destructive potential.

Protesters unable or unwilling to attend the initial meeting joined us. Curious onlookers invaded downtown. Two thousand people filled the main corner of Carbondale's puny downtown district. We sat down, obstructing traffic. We intended to spend several hours blocking routine downtown intercourse. We'd hit the establishment where it hurt—in their pocketbooks.

We talked and sang, laughed and bantered, enjoying each other's energy, glorying in our righteous rebellion. Then the seemingly inevitable occurred. About fifty protesters decided to be more militant and moved to nearby railroad tracks, perhaps fifty feet from the center of the crowd. Leaders of the March cajoled, connived, and pleaded, but the railroad protesters refused to budge. The rest of the crowd nagged and bitched. Still they sat. The police delivered an ultimatum. They'd decided to let us block downtown commerce, but they couldn't tolerate interfering with trains. One would come through downtown in about an hour. The tracks needed to be cleared within thirty minutes. If protesters persisted in remaining on the tracks, they'd be forcibly removed. A few railroad sitters left. A few replacements moved to the tracks and they remained blocked.

The street sitters, proud in our peaceful, rightful protest, began to wonder what would happen. Though nervous we meant to remain. We didn't agree with those idiots who blocked the rails.

We watched and listened to the variety of faces and bodies surrounding us. Most conversations revolved around drugs or sex. Time ticked away. We noticed tanks edging closer. I pulled my light, white jacket from underneath my bottom, hands tensed about the fabric. Bobby and Scott retrieved their protective garb. Tanks pulled nearer. Men in drab, gray-green uniforms stalked toward us. The crowd on the railroad tracks grew feistier. Anxiety pierced the air. An angry, anxious, booming voice matched our mood.

A soldier gripping a megaphone bellowed the time: "Fifteen minutes to clear the tracks!" Yells. Taunts. A few screeching, piercing voices, unaided by megaphones, returned the chatter. A few more people edged over to the tracks. A few others retreated.

HELL NO, WE WON'T GO! HELL NO, WE WON'T GO!

HELL NO, WE WON'T GO!

"Ten minutes to clear the tracks! We are not joking! This is a serious matter! We will forcibly remove you!"

More screams. More challenges. Verbal jousting became a precarious foreplay to the grave business at hand.

HELL NO, WE WON'T GO! HELL NO, WE WON'T GO! HELL NO, WE WON'T GO! HELL NO, WE WON'T GO!

No one from the crowd sitting in the middle of the main street corner, the corner Bobby, Scott and I inhabited, evinced any inclination to move. We were on a mission. We awaited the fate of our rowdier friends. Our chanting continued.

HELL NO, WE WON'T GO! HELL NO, WE WON'T GO! We sang Country Joe and the Fish's anti-war song, the "I-Feel-Like-I'm-Fixin'-To-Die-Rag," which asked why we were fighting and dying in a war in a country on the other side of the world that didn't seem to have a lot to do with our lives, despite the politicians' rhetoric. Then, more chanting: HELL NO, WE WON'T GO! HELL NO, WE WON'T GO! HELL NO, WE WON'T GO! HELL NO, WE WON'T GO! HELL NO, WE WON'T GO!

"Five minutes to clear the tracks! If you do not remove yourselves peaceably, we will be forced to take actions we do not want to use! Measures you will not like. We are concerned about your safety, but we cannot vouch for it! You may get hurt! You may be harmed! Remove yourselves from the tracks! This is your final warning!

HELL NO, WE WON'T GO! HELL NO, WE WON'T GO! HELL NO, WE WON'T GO! HELL NO, WE WON'T GO! HELL

NO, WE WON'T GO! HELL NO, WE WON'T GO!

A few people rose around us. They looked at the soldiers, peered at the tanks. Eyes enlarged with wonder, fear. Some sat. Some remained on their feet. A few walked toward campus. Four minutes remained.

The crowd on the railroad tracks ebbed and flowed. I gazed in that direction and watched a few brave, reckless souls join their companions on the tracks. I looked again and people got up and left. Three minutes remained.

Bobby, Scott, and I eyed one another. The moment of truth. We feared it. We couldn't believe another disaster like Kent State could happen here. Two minutes remained.

HELL NO, WE WON'T GO! HELL NO, WE WON'T GO! HELL NO, WE WON'T GO! HELL NO, WE WON'T GO! HELL NO, WE WON'T GO! HELL NO, WE WON'T GO!

One minute remained.

The soft, low whistle of an oncoming train split the night. Onlookers left. A few stragglers refused to leave the railroad tracks. Hundreds, maybe thousands of others maintained their posts on the corner.

HELL NO, WE WON'T GO! HELL NO, WE WON'T GO! HELL NO, WE WON'T GO! HELL NO, WE WON'T GO! HELL NO, WE WON'T GO! HELL NO, WE WON'T GO!

Metal whizzed beyond us. A thud and a fire ensued. Screams. Flesh sizzled and burned. Smoke filled the air. Tear gas canisters randomly creased the crowd. As a body the mass jumped to its feet, heading home, to campus. Running, screaming, frenzied cries. A few voices made themselves heard.

"Watch out for the canisters." "They're on fire." "Put something over your faces." Many protesters failed to heed the warning about bringing a jacket or handkerchief and coughed and gagged in the night air.

"Bastards!" "Sons-of-bitches!" "Pigs!" "War-mongers!"

I walked along, as calmly as I could. Afraid for my safety but conscious of breaking bones if I forgot myself and ran, I silently counseled patience. "You will get out of here. Be calm. Put one foot in front of another. Don't panic. You've walked these streets hundreds of times. Just move along casually, steadily. You'll make it."

My stiff left leg, confined in its brace, unable to bend at the knee, dragged behind my more anxious, stronger limb. But heeding my advice, walking along as slowly as I could pace myself, as fast as I dared, I saw sights fleeter protesters may have missed.

A metal canister burned on the ground surrounded by a low-grade, almost invisible yellow flame. Found more often by flesh than by sight, yelps and curses reached me as retreating war resisters chanced upon the canisters. Gas hung in the still air. I placed my jacket firmly over my nose and mouth and as close to my eyes as I dared. I'd have closed my eyes altogether and used the jacket to shield my entire face had I not observed so many people running into or narrowly missing tear gas canisters.

Soldiers continued to move toward us as we retreated in the direction of campus. They didn't hurry to catch us, but they did appear miffed. Tear gas canisters continued to be tossed at the crowd. Taunts back and forth between soldiers and protesters nixed any chance at peace. The Guard herded us like cattle back toward campus.

Not all peace protesters retreated tranquilly. Some grabbed rocks and trashed stores. Vandalism began at almost every downtown business, looting evidenced in items being carried away from downtown. The peace protest betrayed by violence. I walked on less self-righteously. Were we no better than the soldiers who'd been turned on us? Were we really serious about peace?

I had lots of time to muse. Bobby and Scott hadn't waited for me. They could run and I couldn't, so why chance getting hurt when they could get out of there? I wasn't completely pleased with this line of thinking, but it did appear realistic, so I agreed to it. But I wanted to know what they thought of the night's events. At length, campus landmarks filtered their way into my subconscious as I moved like an automaton toward my dorm. Frantic voices, jumpy students, laundered the grassy area between the dorms. I didn't see Bobby or Scott.

Knocking at Bobby's dorm room, a chorus of "come in's" greeted me. We'd all been out that night and expressed disbelief at the amount of tear gas tossed our way. Smug in our preparation for that eventuality, we were angry at the unruly segment of the crowd who'd disobeyed our leaders, sat on the railroad tracks and endangered us all. We were more furious with the soldiers who unhesitatingly followed their orders, just like the drones in Vietnam.

Slightly conscious of soldiers who'd followed us towards the dorms, in unison, we all sensed their presence. We smelled tear gas. Looking around, we realized it came from the air-conditioning vents.

Those stupid soldiers gassed the dorm.

Four stories of coughing, hacking, bleary-eyed students exited. Crowds emerged from other dorms. The soldiers, the senseless, silly soldiers not only followed us, but gassed us while we sat silently, harmlessly, in our homes. We were pissed.

We weren't alone. Hundreds, maybe thousands, of people who could have cared less about the war in Vietnam or the night's peace protests had been rudely roused from their crude castles. We began to plan the next night's activities. We wanted back out on the streets. We had no intention of backing down to this tyrannical, military madness.

Classes didn't matter now. We spent the day planning for evening, the third night of demonstrating. We walked toward the area of campus where we'd begun the previous night's events. We strolled past the Armory. Tanks were out, more visible, more menacing than the night before. Guardsmen watched, less likely to be silent than before. Cries of cowards, taunts of pigs. Calmer, gentler souls holding their neighbors on both sides back from attacking one another. We walked on.

Two to three thousand people crowded together that night. Many dorm residents who hadn't appeared the night before joined us, angry at having been gassed.

Campus leaders declared, "We will not be intimidated! We have a viewpoint we intend to convey! We will not be silenced! We will not be afraid! We will end this war!" Anti-war leaders milled around the microphone waiting their turn to exhort the crowd, becoming more passionate and militant with each speech.

Doubts formed. I had no desire to repeat the destruction and looting of the past night, but angry, fired-up speakers urged the crowd to convey our message in any conceivable way. If need be, we'd fight violence with violence. We'd not be intimidated by people wearing uniforms and holding guns. We'd wreck this town if that's what needed to happen.

My stomach churned. I agreed to participate in a peace protest, a non-violent, peace protest. I refused to participate in this travesty. I got up. Bobby and Scott looked at me in wonderment. I explained. Their attention returned to the stage. They stayed with the protest. I left.

I walked to my dorm room, disappointed, dismayed. Why couldn't we do it right? Why couldn't we be different? Why'd we lower ourselves to their level? I seethed inside while lying quietly on my bed.

Unusual night noises penetrated my contemplation. Campus buzzed. I listened to radio reports of the evening's activities. Loud and sometimes abusive, the crowd chose a different target this night. A closer, more vulnerable opponent. SIU's President lived smack dab in the middle of campus. The vocal, potentially violent crowd marched onto the President's lawn and surrounded his house. Anti-war chants sounded, condemning the President, in league with the Guard, for the actions of the previous night, for gassing downtown protesters, for gassing students in their dorms, for being a jerk.

The President implemented a curfew. The crowd ignored it, refusing to leave. The President responded by suspending classes. The quarter had been called off. The crowd, victorious in closing the

University, dispersed.

We had power. We were the wave of the future! I floated on a natural high all night long.

SIU suspended classes on May 12, 1970. I left for home the next day. A day later, and ten days after the deaths of four students at Kent State, tragedy struck again. Two young black men lost their lives and a dozen others were wounded at Jackson State College in Mississippi when police fired into a protesting crowd.

I returned to campus for the summer session. In our dorm, I met Rick. We decided to share a trailer in the fall and enjoyed the space until an early cold snap. The oil tank sitting outside the trailer had yet to be filled for winter. We had no heat.

My body responded in a way I'd never felt before. It was my worst bone crisis. My knee hurt. My hip ached. The chill penetrated my entire body. All I could feel was pain. I didn't go to classes. I didn't leave the trailer. I didn't move from the bed. I whimpered. I screamed. I cursed God. I cried. Suicide began to appeal. Not because I wanted to die, but to do something, anything to escape the pain. Weeks later, when I began to move, I dropped out and returned home to mend. When I came back to campus for winter quarter, I moved into a small apartment building—heat provided.

In May 1971, Bobby, Scott and I climbed a chartered bus to Washington, DC. Thousands descended on the nation's capitol for an anti-war demonstration. One of the largest demonstrations in U.S. history, thousands of protesters were arrested to stymie plans to shut down the city. Sitting in the midst of the crowd spanning the lawn from the Capitol to the Lincoln Memorial, I felt frustrated. I came to protest the war. I could live with joints snaking through the crowd, but not with those whose sole intent was to party or who showed up because it was the hip thing to do. Some came for peace; others to carouse.

Speakers echoed the rhetoric that repelled me a year before. We were encouraged, cajoled, and commanded to do whatever was necessary to end the war. Violence meted out to our oppressors to end violence was justifiable as long as it ended the war. The argument mystified me—how could violence foster peace?

I decided to study revolutions: American, French, and Russian. I'd become a historian who'd understand how to stimulate radical, successful change. Without wavering from this decision, I packed my bags that summer for Tucson, Arizona, where I'd start my junior year in the warm climate my body craved.

Chapter 6:

Sun, Love, and Pain

January 31, 1975

To: John H. Saiki, University of New Mexico, School of Medicine

At this time, we have no active program in which we study the progression of Gaucher's Disease in young adults. Unfortunately, there are a large number of such patients and we usually reserve our attention for patients with either severe or unusual manifestations of the disease. There is at this time no satisfactory treatment of such patients.

Howard R. Sloan, M.D., Ph.D., Molecular Disease Branch, National Institutes of Health

The desert sun radiated smiles into my bones. I walked, metal-free, along Tucson's University of Arizona (UA) campus majoring in history and political science. My new orthopedic physician met no objection when he suggested relinquishing my hip-length brace, fearing the alleviation of weight off my left hip would be offset by atrophying leg muscles.

The sun glowed in geology class, too, where a petite woman caught my eye. More than a foot shorter than me, sporting flowing, light brown hair cascading to her waist, I noticed Gloria right away, but said only "hi" until the middle of the semester. Then we had a project together. She majored in anthropology, a field I didn't know much about. I wanted to ask her out, but didn't find the courage until late in the semester when chances began to narrow.

On an early date we attended a basketball game. Within weeks we spent all our free time together. Both of us anticipated parting during the Christmas break to assess our feelings.

I boarded a bus to Phoenix to visit my snowbird grandparents. I woke one morning recalling a dream I'd had in Carbondale of an apartment room I'd never seen. At the time I'd dismissed it as imagination. But the memory of the size of the room, the color of dresser drawers, and the shade of drapes made me realize I slept in the room I'd dreamt about. How, I wondered, could a place I'd never seen appear in a dream?

These thoughts paled to ones about my relationship. Did we have a future? How would my family react when they discovered she wasn't Jewish? How would I respond to their reactions? So much to consider. Back to Tucson.

Acing my history and political science finals, the next semester's classes moved along smoothly. Gloria and I continued to date. We spent lots of time sunning outdoors, reading textbooks and novels ensconced among many other students on the grassy areas between buildings. We shared passions for going to the movies and sampling nearby restaurants.

One evening we brought a blanket to a nearby park. We lie there smooching when we heard a strange noise. Suddenly, sprinklers showered us. We laughed at our plight and hastened back to campus. We happily contemplated a future together.

Visiting my family in Illinois at spring break my parents expressed dismay, but not surprise that I'd chosen to be with someone who wasn't Jewish. I listened in disbelief when one of them said they'd believed it likely I'd find someone of another faith because I "blamed Judaism for my disease." I'd never had such a thought and wondered where that came from. Despite our tensions my parents planned their next summer vacation to travel to Arizona to meet their future daughter-in-law and see my new home.

That same summer I discovered the effectiveness of a quiet protest. I worked at one of the University libraries. I loved the job and my boss but I had a conversation with her one day that infuriated me. The Library dress code prohibited men, but not women, from wearing shorts during the hot summer months. I wondered what to do about this injustice?

I walked into the Library one early summer day wearing shorts. My boss glanced my way, silently conveying both frustration and bemusement, then looked away. She, too, disputed the Code's double standard. My quiet protest gained momentum when a couple of others joined me. The code changed. The irony of my protest was the library's air conditioning worked so effectively I couldn't keep wearing shorts because I got too cold. But I discovered rules could be modified without fanfare and reform implemented even if it happened so quietly no one remembered a change occurred.

As a senior and one year ahead of Gloria I planned to graduate in the spring of 1973, then stay in Tucson at least one more year working at whatever job I could find. I hoped to live in Tucson for the rest of my life, but for that to occur I needed to leave. Having decided to pursue a doctorate in history and become a professor, any hope of being hired at UA depended on attending a different graduate school. The school refused to hire its own graduates to avoid inbred scholarship. I worked at various jobs while Gloria finished her senior year and we planned our wedding.

We held a June ceremony in Gloria's family's suburban Phoenix backyard. The grass shimmered. All my immediate relatives traveled to Arizona to celebrate. Both sets of grandparents. Aunts and uncles. My parents and brother and sister. Our Tucson friends. Gloria's family. Rows of people waited for the mid-afternoon nuptials. I anticipated its end. I wanted to get going. I became edgier after my maternal grandmother fainted. It seemed she always drew attention to herself. This was supposed to be our day. I couldn't believe the heat was that bad. After all, it was only June—it wouldn't get really hot until July or August.

Finally, we were officially married! Our guests indulged themselves in the post-matrimonial festivities. I wanted to leave. We changed clothes, got in our Valiant, trailing streamers and cans from our rear bumper, with "Just Married" painted on the back window, and started our honeymoon drive to the eastern border of Arizona and New Mexico.

This particular trip appealed because in the fall I'd enter graduate school working towards my Master's Degree in history at New Mexico State University (NMSU) in southern New Mexico. Las Cruces, soon to be our new home, lay only 20 miles north of the Mexican border.

I'd stayed healthier during my three years in Tucson than ever before, with no bone crises, though an underlying chronic pain persisted. When it intensified I swallowed prescription painkillers. As we readied to leave Tucson my body disintegrated with a bone crisis unlike any before. While the intense pain didn't last as long the episode lingered beyond the traditional two-week period and into our time to move east.

Gloria did the bulk of the packing and friends helped us load our car and a small U-Haul trailer. We bid farewell to Tucson one late July afternoon. Unable to drive myself, Gloria drove the 200 miles through steep, mountainous roads. When we arrived in Las Cruces in the middle of the night we stumbled into our new home. The next morning, still hurting, I began unloading the U-Haul. It was the least I could do.

Slowly regaining my strength in our first few weeks in Las Cruces, I didn't realize how impactful emotional changes, such as matrimony, could adversely affect my health. Or how a series of events, like moving, changing jobs, and starting graduate school, on top of getting married, might be psychologically devastating. Fortunately, other distractions appeared.

While classes started, Gloria needed to work. Unsure of what she wanted to do next academically and ready for a break from school, she found a job as a phlebotomist, drawing blood. We could now pay rent and buy food.

NMSU, a school of about 10,000 students, was half the size of my two previous universities. I connected with my fellow students and professors, an impressive group of committed teachers and serious historians, noted in fields from European to South American to U.S. history. This atmosphere fit my needs perfectly as reflected in

"A" grades.

I'd have been completely happy toward the end of my first semester, except we ran out of money. I prepared to drop out of school, find work, re-build our savings, and then return to school. Before putting this plan into action the History Department Chair called me into his office to discuss my future and I shared my intentions. When he heard I planned to drop out he wondered if being a Graduate Assistant would make a difference. I jumped at the offer.

When we arrived in Las Cruces I walked or biked the few blocks to school while Gloria drove to the hospital. Near the end of my first semester I relinquished my bike because pedaling hurt my knees. My newest physician suggested trying Demerol, a morphine derivative, to alleviate what had turned into constant above-the-surface pain since my last bone crisis in Tucson. It became the first drug to noticeably minimize my pain.

My doctor knew little about GD and he suggested using the winter break to be evaluated by a physician at the University of New Mexico School of Medicine in Albuquerque. This physician echoed all the others, unable to predict my future. Despite chronic pain and acute bone crises the hardest part of having GD remained not knowing what to expect.

In school, I persisted in my goal to learn how revolutions worked. The most instructive class to that end concerned the Russian Revolution. I read Lenin's text, *What Is to Be Done?*, internalizing many of his ideas, including the ability of a small, dedicated band of individuals to incite change. This fit my UA Library dress code experience. One day I hoped to put my learning into practice on a broader scale.

After two years in Las Cruces we anticipated my 1976 graduation and doctoral education. After applying to several schools, and this time ensuring an assistantship prior to relocating, I enrolled at the University of Oklahoma in Norman, about twenty miles south of Oklahoma City. Neither one of us had been to that state before.

Chapter 7:

Genes and James

30 September 1977

To: Dr. Peter Grozea, Oklahoma Medical Research Foundation

Dear Dr. Grozea:

Your patient, Steven Brown, and his wife were recently in Chicago and requested fibroblast testing to determine whether or not Mrs. Brown was a carrier of Gaucher's disease....Mrs. Brown is not a carrier of the gene for the disease. Thus, they are not at risk of having children affected with Gaucher's disease. All of their children, however, will be carriers.

Barbara K. Burton, M.D., Division of Genetics,

Children's Memorial Hospital

Norman, a town of 60,000 to 70,000 inhabitants, sat in the plains of central Oklahoma. Before school began I met my engaging advisor, an American intellectual historian. I'd specialize in this field, studying the evolution of ideas, emphasizing the period between the American Revolution and World War I when many reform movements entered the collective consciousness. As his Teaching Assistant I'd be responsible for leading discussion classes and grading students.

I nervously awaited my first day in the classroom. Would I

be accepted or have enough material to fill fifty minutes? How would I, extremely shy, facilitate a group of 30 students?

I walked into my classroom for the first time and dumped my materials on the front desk. The room quieted. I didn't have to do or say anything. My first experience with position power. Hiding my relief I moved forward and began to enjoy engaging in the class-room—but my physical pace continued to wane.

Arthritis had recently been diagnosed as a secondary condi-tion to GD, especially in my hips and knees. An orthopedic surgeon told me the pain and necrosis in my left hip signaled the need for an eventual hip replacement. I acknowledged his diagnosis. My basic approach to GD was to ignore it as much as possible. I did what the doctors told me, ingested drugs to minimize the pain, and got on with life.

In 1977, Gloria and I had been married for three years and together for five. I'd long ago concluded I wouldn't be responsible for bringing a baby with GD into this world, refusing to inflict such pain on an innocent child. While any child I helped conceive would harbor the GD gene, as a carrier they wouldn't have the disease it-self. We needed to be certain Gloria wasn't a carrier herself before planning a pregnancy. Several hospitals around the country offered genetic tests that could make that determination.

We scheduled a late-summer vacation around the opportunity to take the genetic test at the University of Chicago, while also visit-ing my parents to celebrate my Mom's 50th birthday. A few weeks after the test my doctor would receive the results.

We learned Gloria didn't have the GD gene, shortly after my

second year in the doctoral program began, and within a month or two we announced a pregnancy. Needing a bigger place to live for a family of three we found a small three-bedroom house.

I taught intersession classes between semesters as part of my constant search to supplement my assistantship income. These classes collapsed an entire semester into a couple of weeks. At the start of one intersession I felt that familiar twinge. Soon immersed in the pain of a bone crisis I despaired. I'd already begun teaching, but now I couldn't move. Purchasing a tape recorder, I sucked in my breath, then through the fog of pain and drugs daily recorded my lectures. Gloria brought the tape recorder to class each day. With contemporary technology, this solution is unimaginable, but in the late 1970s, cordless phones, personal computers, or the Internet, had yet to appear. Looking back I don't know how any of us did it—myself, my wife, or my students—but we did.

Recovering from this episode, I used crutches or a cane to limp around. My orthopedist insisted I'd need a hip replacement one day but stressed waiting as long as possible. Medical science would become more sophisticated and no one knew how my fragile bones would react to this surgery. Since hip replacements didn't last a lifetime the longer I waited the better my chances to outlive an artificial hip. I continued biding my time, ingesting Demerol, and living with constant, fairly intense pain, which I thought I did a decent job of ignoring.

I'd also started seeing a hematologist, a physician who was an expert at analyzing blood-related issues, at the University of Oklahoma (OU) Medical School. She facilitated lab work every few months and monitored my condition, expressing increasing concern at the growth of my spleen and liver. I did my best to ignore her and live a normal life.

We created a nursery in the bedroom opposite our own at one end of our small house, joined a Lamaze class, toured the hospital's maternity ward, watched movies about births, and practiced breathing exercises.

As the months clicked forward, I prepared for my comprehensive exams. One Saturday evening toward the end of July sitting at the kitchen table, timer ticking while working on a take-home test for one of my last classes, Gloria walked into the room with a strange look on her face. Her water broke. I pushed aside my papers, called the doctor, finished packing last minute essentials, and drove carefully and deliberately to the hospital, just as instructed. A long night began.

We knew first labors tended to be lengthy. My job consisted of ensuring Gloria remained as comfortable as possible. That meant providing water, ice chips, breathing exercises, and whatever else she might need, but no one warned me how bored I'd be after hours of sitting in a hospital chair awaiting the birth. We tried everything—talking, games, TV—but I couldn't stay awake.

Finally, after twelve hours of labor, we welcomed Aimée Elizabeth Brown into the world on July 23, 1978. Her first name honored Gloria's French heritage. The initial "E" and the name Elizabeth paid tribute to my maternal grandmother, Edna.

Holding this tiny creature I'd helped create in my arms, I carried her to Gloria, who glanced at her and commented, "She looks like a monkey." Mortified, I wanted to seize my daughter and cradle her in my arms, but I lacked what the baby needed.

I'd planned to be an equal partner in the raising of our child, now the apple of her mother's eye, but my weak hip and knees rebelled. Even at the tiniest of weights lifting Aimée hurt. Within months I knew my body could handle only one child.

Depending more often now on my cane to relieve pressure from my left hip, I found rides to campus, eschewing preferred walks. Irritability and anger intensified as pain and immobility increased. "What's wrong?" friends often asked, puzzling me with their queries. I refused to believe my countenance betrayed my inner turmoil. I ignored my pain; why did others keep bringing it to the forefront?

Immersed in reading to prepare for my exams in early 1979, Gloria and I agreed I'd get up about four or five in the morning so I could read for an hour or two before Aimée awoke. When she did I'd give her a bottle, enjoying father-daughter time, while Gloria caught up on sleep.

I poured myself into passing my exams, which would lead to dissertation and graduation. I didn't ace them, but I did pass, the most important thing. A few days of celebration ensued then I began to concentrate on finding a dissertation topic. I wanted to write about an individual but not a traditional biography. My advisor suggested Henry James, Sr., who I knew little about, though I'd read materials by his sons—Henry, the novelist, and William, considered the founder of American psychology.

I learned James, Sr. also had a prominent father, William

James of Albany, an entrepreneur and financier of the Erie Canal. Born in 1811, Henry James, Sr. lost a leg at the age of thirteen. I'd "discovered" a man who'd suffered physical hardship, which I might comprehend differently than another historian. He led a life of the mind as a writer and speaker, fitting my field of American intellectual history, and his life spanned much of the nineteenth century, meeting my chronological focus. Researchers had access to volumes of James's papers and letters housed in various repositories in the Boston area. I'd spend a week there in my upcoming spring break. I'd found my man.

James lost his leg playing a game called "fireball," where a globe of flax was soaked in turpentine, then ignited and kicked. This particular ball snaked into a barn. The thirteen year-old James helped stamp out the resulting fire, injuring his leg in the process. He suffered through two painful amputations, one below and one above the knee--prior to the discovery of anesthesia--spending two years in bed recovering from these operations.

Wealthy from his inheritance he pursued his own intellectual and spiritual paths without money worries. He became a non-traditional follower of Emanuel Swedenborg, a European scientist turned mystic who lived from 1688 to 1772. In his mid-fifties, Swedenborg experienced a mystical visit from "the Lord" who informed the scientist he'd be guided to reveal the spiritual meaning of the Bible. James immersed himself in Swedenborg's work, publishing numerous books with his own spin on the beliefs.

In Boston, I'd visit Harvard's Houghton Library, the Boston Public Library, and a Swedenborgian church and study center in the suburb of Newton, all of which had James' repositories. Preparing for this trip, my hip now ached constantly and I packed crutches as well as my suitcase. Boarding the plane like a "real" historian, ready to dig through archival papers my excitement overshadowed pain. Once I arrived and started the actual work I realized one week didn't provide the necessary time to review all of James's papers. I returned to Norman considering ways to return to Boston for an extended stay.

The summer of 1980 approached. I'd turn twenty-nine in the fall and intended to graduate in May 1981, before my thirtieth birthday.

After receiving research grants fostering a longer trip to Boston a new set of problems and questions arose. Where would I stay for a visit of six weeks? Could Gloria and Aimée get to Boston for short holiday? Would I want to re-visit Dr. Crocker at Boston's Children's Hospital? How would I get around lugging suitcases and other paraphernalia?

I learned I had a distant cousin who owned a large house in Cambridge. They'd be vacationing during much of my planned time in the area and I could stay there.

The intensifying pain in my hip, I learned between my two current Boston trips, resulted from cartilage being stripped away from cushioning bone, leading to one bone grinding into another. When moving in just the "right" way, the pain in my hip stole my breath, literally stopping me in my tracks.

By the time summer arrived and I deplaned in Boston my body slumped compared to my visit only a few months before. Descending on my cousin's house in Cambridge I walked into a mansion-like structure, complete with flights of stairs. They asked if I could navigate the house? Assuring them it'd work out, in retrospect I wonder if they worried about me injuring myself in their home? But we all adjusted and they left for their vacation while I concentrated on work. By the time Gloria and Aimée arrived stacks of notepapers and photocopies filled my suitcase.

One day we got in a cab bound for Dr. Crocker's office for a late afternoon appointment. My crutches partially relieved pain that had now moved to both my ankles. While Dr. Crocker seemed happy to see me and meet my family, he didn't conceal his worry about my health. With little to offer in the way of news about GD, he simply encouraged us to move forward with our lives.

Back home, I'd abandoned my cane to use my crutches at all times. Intense bone pain persisted and after a shopping trip we learned to our dismay the simple act of walking had caused a hairline fracture in my right hip. My doctor warned me about doing too much, reminding me to be cautious and pace myself. Instead I used Demerol to allay the pain.

I taught and worked on my dissertation. Over Christmas break we traveled to California to visit Gloria's sister and her family in San Jose. One day Gloria's mom and sister babysat while the rest of us explored the area. When we got back Aimée sat in a corner. Gloria's mom told us Aimée had been sitting in front of the Christmas tree playing when she started swearing up a storm, repeating "shit, shit, shit" numerous times. Gloria's Mom thought it funny, but her sister was appalled and wondered where Aimée would hear such language. Gloria and I looked at each other--we knew.

Leaving the airport parking lot on our way home from this trip we wrote a check as usual to pay the parking fee, but at the booth the attendant informed us checks were no longer accepted. We didn't have enough cash and had yet to use credit cards. I started arguing. The attendant sensing my resolution asked us to move our car away from the tollbooth and speak to the manager. My temper roared. As soon as we parked I confronted the manager, declaring they could take a check or we could drive away. There was no alternative.

I didn't recognize myself. The shy man tentative about speaking up in class, the person who feared how students might react the first time he entered the front of a classroom, just laid down the law. Backing down didn't occur. I meant my ultimatum. The manager took our check and I returned to the car a changed man, my wife staring at a stranger.

Chapter 8:

Overnight Radical

April 7, 1981
   Mr. Steven Brown
   Dear Steve:
I hope you continue to recover from the operation.
The platelet count was slightly higher than at discharge.
   Sylvia Bottomley, Professor of Medicine
   University of Oklahoma-Health Sciences Center

I worked in the library putting the finishing touches on "Henry James Sr. and the American Experience" in the spring semester of 1981. One day a lady I'd seen many times got onto the elevator with me. We nodded and I looked away. She frightened me. Scrunched into a wheelchair, scarred and twisted fingers jutting from a knobby elbow she pushed a similarly knotted cane above her and rapped the elevator button. I imagined her smacking my fingers. I knew she was a doctoral student in English and we had traits in common—but I didn't care to explore them.

I'd regressed a great deal in the year since my last Boston trip. Walking the short distance from the History building parking lot to the campus library created excruciating bone pain and exhaustion. I applied for a Handicapped Parking placard. Its arrival served as a respite for my crumbling body's dwindling reserves of energy and frustration. Walking to campus receded into my past; now I drove from one parking lot to another. I'd become officially "handi-capped."

At the same time, ominous blood tests superseded attention to my bones. The lower left side of my stomach bulged like a displaced pregnancy as my spleen absorbed multitudes of Gaucher cells and other cells as well, causing my platelet and white blood cell counts to sink to abnormally, dangerously low levels accelerating anemia and explaining my decreasing energy. Doctors wondered how I managed to stay healthy but I rarely felt ill—with the exception of periodic bone breaks and constant pain. Still, with my blood counts at dangerously low levels, all the doctors recommended the removal of my spleen.

Would the recommended removal of this organ mean surplus Gaucher cells would find another home? No one knew, but doctors concluded the spleen had to go—leaving it in and letting it grow risked deleteriously low, potentially life-threatening, blood counts.

My March 1981 splenectomy removed a fourteen pound (thirteen pounds above average) spleen riddled with Gaucher cells. A picture of my former internal organ appeared in at least one medical textbook of the time describing GD.

My blood counts increased after the splenectomy, but so did my pain. An orthopedic physician in Oklahoma City observed my deteriorating right hip "looked worse than any other GD hip" he'd seen. Concurring with my local doctor he cautioned against a hip replacement until I could no longer stand the pain. "What", I wanted to know, "constituted too much pain?" The answer: "when you can't sleep through the night without medication then it's time." That had yet to happen, so I continued my daily routine of an anti-inflammatory drug to prevent serious joint swelling and multiple doses of painkillers

Two months after my operation, diploma in hand, I didn't know what I'd do with my life. It was a terrible time to seek employment in any of the social sciences because older Baby Boomers filled positions throughout the country. The History Department, recognizing the hopelessness of this situation, hired one recent graduate a year to teach American history survey courses with the hope a transition year would enable a graduate to secure an academic position. I filled the position in its second year.

I sat in a chair throwing a Frisbee at a graduation party when my back started to hurt. I assumed I'd pulled a muscle, but the ache didn't subside. Initial X-rays revealed no cause for the pain. Weeks later, with reduced but persistent pain, a newer X-ray revealed a fractured, almost healed, vertebrae in my lower back, reminiscent of my first hip fracture. I'd never had any bone involvement above my waist until this appeared. It seemed to result from the splenectomy.

Undeterred I became a History Instructor in Fall 1981, lecturing to classes of 300 or more. Unable to stand or walk around, I perched my butt on the stage to deliver lectures. I discovered an ability to project my voice without using a microphone and learned over time how often I appeared mild-mannered until people heard my "loud" voice.

At the end of a class on my first day of teaching two students approached me requesting permission to tape my lectures. One was blind; another had a visual impairment. Attempting to bond I mentioned getting around using a cane or crutches. We began talking about subjects other than history. I learned about a new organization called the Independent Living Project (ILP), whose staff advocated for the integration of people with disabilities in all aspects of life, including housing, transportation, and employment. The ILP encouraged individuals with disabilities to share their life experiences to help each other figure out how to live in a world designed for non-disabled people.

The students wondered if I'd consider attending a meeting and volunteering for the organization. Out of politeness I agreed. In my experience people at meetings sat around discussing many topics but rarely accomplished anything. I left the room amazed. The ILP staff planned a statewide conference to introduce people to its existence and educate us about a variety of disability issues, including sexuality. I said I'd give volunteering a try.

My year as an Instructor ended without a job in sight. I sat home reading one summer day, not knowing what else to do, when my department chair called. A representative of a Tulsa-based association asked him to recommend someone to write their organizational history. "Would I be interested?" Though it had nothing to do with my field it offered a paycheck and I immediately placed a call to the association's contact. Over the phone, my contact declared he was "impressed because I'd completed my dissertation more quickly than anyone else he'd known, himself included." He encouraged me to write a book proposal. In the next couple of weeks, we continued to discuss the proposal over the phone. He liked my narrative and assisted me with budgets, which I knew nothing about. I sent the entire proposal to the association and my contact called to tell me I'd been hired.

Shortly after our verbal agreement, my contact called again, saying he'd be traveling from Tulsa to Dallas and had a layover for a couple of hours in Oklahoma City. "Could we meet?" Eager to please, I explained I'd be easy to spot since I was 6'4," had a beard, and used crutches. As soon as he heard the word "crutches" he wanted to know "what was wrong?" I felt no discomfort in describing my GD history. He listened and we then arranged our meeting.

Sweat leaked onto my crutch handles when I walked into the airport to meet my future employer. In those days, before security prevented someone from walking to a gate, I met my contact for the first time and we sat down in one of the airport restaurants. My nerves didn't seem to bother the handsome, intense man with stylish brown hair and glasses. I don't recall the specifics of the conversation, but I know I didn't feel great about it, sensing my anxiety might have derailed me if we hadn't already communicated so much by phone. At the end, I guessed I did okay because when we parted he said he'd notify me in a few days when to travel to Tulsa during an upcoming week to meet the rest of the company and finalize a written contract.

I sat by the phone for a call that never came. After an excruciating week, I sucked in my breath and called my contact. He told me "the company had changed their mind." After discussing it they'd decided someone using crutches couldn't write the book they had in mind. Astounded and unable to let this go, I questioned this reasoning in a forty-five minute conversation. All I recall, thirty years later, is "maybe if you had the physique of a football player, you'd possess the stamina to do the job," but since I was a skinny, unathletic looking guy, using crutches, they questioned my ability and energy to complete the research, travel, and writing required.

Steaming mad, I slammed down the phone, got in my car and drove to the ILP to recreate this conversation. I wanted to know what I could do about this blatant discrimination. I learned no laws protected people with disabilities from being discriminated against, but I refused to hear this response. I called several other organizations, ranting about my experience. Everyone concurred I'd encountered discrimination, but it wasn't illegal. Desperate, I met with a lawyer who acknowledged the inequity but because it was not against the law she couldn't pursue a remedy.

My final stop was the state Human Rights Commission. A staff member listened to my complaint, processed the appropriate paperwork, and let me know a decision would be shared within six months. About seven or eight months later I learned their investigation concluded yes I'd been discriminated against on the basis of my disability, but since no law prevented that from happening they too could offer no recourse.

I became radicalized overnight into a disability rights advocate.

Chapter 9:

Fitting In and Laying Down

November 10, 1983

DISCHARGE SUMMARY

The patient's past medical history is all associated with Gaucher's disease. Surgical history includes tonsillectomy and adenoidectomy at age sixteen [sic], splenectomy at age thirty, placement of Harrington rods in June of 1983.

G. Rainey Williams, M.D., Professor of Surgery

S. E. Dakil, M.D., Resident, General Surgery

University of Oklahoma-Health Sciences Center

While awaiting the Human Rights Commission decision I volunteered daily at the Independent Living Project. Not long after hearing their decision, toward summer's end, we learned about funding to create two new positions and I applied for one. I'd demonstrated commitment by my constant volunteerism. And I'd begun to understand my ability to research, write, and speak held more value outside the University environment than within it where everyone shared these proficiencies. My potential new boss still had questions, of which the most pertinent concerned comfort, my own and others. How would I feel about working with individuals who, for example, drooled when they talked, or spit, or couldn't control spasms, or needed to communicate through a sign-language interpreter, or walked into walls because they couldn't see, or weren't as intellectually gifted as me? In other words, would I fit in?

I didn't know if this would be an issue, but I understood I had much to learn. A few months before I'd unquestionably have balked at being around such individuals, but based on my summer of volunteering I now thought if I had a problem I'd talk with someone about it and hopefully adjust.

Hired in the fall of 1982, my new job would entail providing consumer skills training, peer support, and community organizing. During the summer I'd learned about a disability paradigm called the "medical model." Doctors and other health care professionals learned during their schooling that people with disabilities suffered from conditions requiring either repair, such as broken bones, or cure, like finding ways to eliminate Muscular Dystrophy or GD. No middle ground existed between being well or sick.

The disability rights movement introduced new paradigms, explaining disability as a long-term condition requiring neither repair nor cure. The mere fact of having a disability didn't equate to misery or needing fixing or meaning we were "in-valid." We may live our lives differently because of disabling conditions, but that didn't signify being any better or worse off than someone without a disability. We discussed the need for our external environments to change so individuals with disabilities could more easily maneuver through our society, not the reverse.

How these paradigms played out became apparent during my first night on the job when I attended a meeting, with three of my colleagues, that became a battlefield. Oklahoma planned to construct sheltered workshops throughout the state, with Norman next on the list. Sheltered workshops were segregated work settings. We advocated integration. To make matters worse, individuals with disabilities working in these workshops usually received payment far below minimum wage for doing piecework, while those running the workshops often earned substantial profits.

The ILP's Board of Directors, United Cerebral Palsy of Cleveland County (UCP-CC), supported the plan to establish a sheltered workshop in Norman. My co-workers did not. They wondered "why would anyone support these workshops? Not only do we know they don't work, but they just reinforce separating people with disabilities from other workers."

This conflict spurred me to ask questions about our Board that hadn't seemed important before. The twenty-plus Board members included parents of individuals with disabilities; professionals who worked mostly with kids with disabilities; some who shared both categories; and two individuals with disabilities. Many Board members joined the organization hoping to find or create support for their growing children. Early in 1981, UCP-CC sought funding to build a wheelchair-accessible housing complex for people with disabilities, especially their own kids.

Helen Kutz, a quadriplegic from a car accident who then served on the Board, cautioned the group about developing housing without providing services for residents. Otherwise, what would be the difference between living at home and elsewhere? She shared information about independent living centers springing up around the country. Despite the name, these weren't residential complexes. Independent living centers usually received enough funding to rent small office space where staff led advocacy efforts and organized services designed to teach individuals with disabilities as well as others in the community how people with disabilities could achieve full integration.

Helen suggested UCP-CC submit a grant application for independent living funds. The Board asked Helen to write a proposal. UCP-CC became the first organization in Oklahoma to provide independent living services. In September 1981, about the time I met the two students in my class who introduced me to independent living, the ILP first opened its doors.

Hired as Executive Director, Helen refused to call the program an Independent Living Center, the preferred name, because the organization didn't consist of a majority of individuals with disabilities. In the late 1970s and early 1980s, people with disabilities used this standard, "consumer control," to judge who actually ran independent living programs. The term "consumer" indicated people with disabilities consumed services, intentionally used to show that individuals with disabilities could be more than someone's charity recipient.

I loved working at the ILP, understanding now how my life made sense within the context of disability rights, combining my passions for justice and reform within a personally relevant movement. No longer the white guy interested in civil rights or the man interested in women's issues, I'd become an individual with a disability advocating for my own people.

Socializing with my new colleagues and their friends introduced many people with disabilities into our household. I even connected with Nan, the woman I'd avoided in the library. One day she confronted me. "I know why you always ducked me. You didn't want anyone to think you were like me." She'd nailed me. Then she saved me. "But I got it. You didn't want to be seen as helpless. You didn't want people to think you couldn't do anything." "Yes," I agreed, "you're right." Then she skillfully placed my reluctance to engage with her into the context of ingrained, negative beliefs about disability.

My wife, Gloria, expressed distress with my newfound life and those who peopled it and wondered how it would impact Aimée. I thought our daughter could only benefit from having broadened horizons.

About this time my parents shared an ad they'd clipped from *Hadassah* magazine. Rubin Bakin had GD and sought pen pals. Rubin filled a void, compiling a newsletter sharing personal experiences with GD and any information he could locate about our rare disease. His blue-inked mimeographed pages helped build a community since most of us had never met or spoken with another person with GD. In my new job, educating myself about peer support—people with disabilities serving as role models and support persons for others with disabilities—I recognized the comparable efforts Rubin provided in his efforts. His work energized me and I asked if he'd be interested in publishing an article about independent living. In 1982 he published "Independent Living-A Concept, A Reality."

I never laughed more than with our small ILP office staff of six, but my enthusiasm for my new job matched an equal depression about my deteriorating health. One day, late in 1982 or early in

1983, Gloria and I made love and my back crackled—another fractured vertebra. This one turned ugly. Within days I lay in agony, immobilized, multiplying my usual doses of narcotics. I cried out often, unable to move any part of my body without antagonizing some muscle, joint, or bone. Relieving my pain became my greatest goal.

I remained in bed. I avoided Aimée because jostling the bed made me flinch. Everything caused pain—nothing alleviated it.

Work ebbed from consciousness. I thanked my lucky stars I'd found a job where my boss understood pain and disability. She encouraged me to take the time I needed and do whatever necessary to recover. Pain became my only constant.

Gloria made an appointment at my orthopedic physician's office and somehow got me there. He immediately consulted my hematologist who recommended I see a neurosurgeon who in turn wanted to perform a spinal myelogram to determine the damage to my back. But he didn't insist. If I consented to the procedure, he said "dye would be injected into my spine and I'd be placed prone on a table that tilted and positioned me upright in a standing position. While it slowly revolved pictures would be taken." I declined.

Intuitively distrusting any physicians in the Oklahoma City area with the current status of my back I recalled conversations with my hematologist about GD research becoming a priority at the National Institutes of Health (NIH). I sought to be touched by only the best doctors and informed my hematologist I wanted to go to NIH. She arranged a trip to Washington.

In spring 1983, a friend drove Gloria and me to the airport. I could barely keep it together to get into a borrowed wheelchair and then in our car. Leg muscles, atrophied from lack of use, started to spasm. I lay in the back seat, yelping at every bump in the road.

We arrived at the airport and managed to get to our gate where an attendant informed us this particular plane wouldn't use a Jetway. Our friend exploded, insisting a Jetway be brought to this gate or the plane be moved to one that did. Airport personnel resisted, but he refused to budge. They relented at last. Getting on the plane I didn't much care what else happened. Maybe when we arrived at NIH relief would be in sight.

When we got there the doctors took one look at me and asked how I'd been able to make the journey at all? Little feeling remained in my legs after hours of travel. The spasticity had intensified. The doctors examined me, poked and prodded, stuck pins in my legs to see where I retained feeling, sedated me, and put me to bed.

The next day, no longer permitted to choose, I lay on a gurney being rolled toward a spinal myelogram. After injecting dye into my spine, orderlies lifted me onto a tilting table. Imagine standing on your head while someone pushes you as hard as they can into the ground, then consider the earth noticeably spinning. That's how being on the tilting table felt, but that was joy compared to the torture of the gurney rides when every bump and crevice shocked like multiple electric blasts.

The myelogram revealed at least two fractured vertebrae. NIH couldn't provide appropriate care. The physicians decided to transfer me to Massachusetts General Hospital (Mass General) in Boston to see expert orthopedic physicians.

A few days later we boarded an air ambulance to Boston. I anticipated a short ride, based on my recent travel to this city that now seemed part of my life, but I was mistaken. I lay strapped immobile, staring at a ceiling only a few feet above me. I didn't think I'd ever been so bored, laying like this for hours, wondering what my future would hold. The four or five hour ride seemed endless.

After we landed in Boston paramedics carefully transferred me into a conventional ambulance. Following more poking, stabbing, and sticking at Mass General, doctors prepared me for surgery in a few days, as soon as I regained some strength. Drugs continued to be administered. Between exhaustion, pain, and medication the next few days passed in a stupor. I remember waking only to watch episodes of *M*A*S*H* and inquire when I'd have the surgery.

When the day finally arrived doctors installed Harrington rods, round steel columns, on both sides of my spinal column and added cow bone to my disintegrating spine to strengthen my crumbing vertebrae. During the surgery an additional bone broke, resulting in the rod on my left side being higher than the one on the right.

After recuperating in intensive care I was wheeled into a room and placed on a Stryker bed. This device contains straps to immobilize the entire body, preventing movement that might cause further injury, especially when the bed is periodically turned over to prevent pressure sores. After a few days, hospital personnel released my arms, but every other part of my body remained confined.

At home, my father had traveled from Illinois to Oklahoma to be with Aimée. Gloria couldn't stay with me indefinitely and both my mother and sister arranged to journey from their Midwestern homes to offer support, trying to ensure the presence of at least one family member at all times.

Lying in that hospital bed within the same four walls day after day I asked myself why? Why had my body punished me all my life?

I unexpectedly found myself reevaluating my core beliefs. Many visitors brought flowers to enliven the room. The more I watched the flowers by my bedside the more they transformed into a metaphor for all of life's beauty.

One day it dawned on me. My body, wracked with breaks and bruises, started to feel different. I thought about athletes experiencing injury after injury and returning to the playing field. I realized on a different, more crucial battlefield, that of life, my body had performed amazing feats.

I started counting. At least six fractures: a broken leg…numerous bone crises…a broken hip…walking for a couple of years with a hip brace…bone crises…a broken hip…ankle problems…knee problems…joint problems…splenectomy…walking with a cane…walking with crutches…broken vertebra…broken vertebrae…who knows what I forgot.

I lay in that hospital bed and began to smile. My body was astounding. For years I'd despaired when I looked into a mirror at my atrophying muscles and imagined lost opportunities. Now I observed a body surviving repeated tests—pushed to its limits on a daily basis. I shouldn't be contemptuous of my body—I should be proud. My body survived incredible hardships. It hit me again—I had an amazing body. Disability didn't necessarily signify weakness;

it could also be seen as a sign of strength.

Suddenly life became a gift, not a burden. For as long as I could recall I'd viewed death as a welcome relief from the pain of this life. I wasn't suicidal, like when I'd lain in pain in my Carbondale trailer, but I hadn't enjoyed living either. I'd had a decent life, so whenever the Grim Reaper wanted me I'd be pleased to go. That attitude now changed. I realized simple pleasures, like flowers by my bedside, helped me feel good about the world. While I'd achieved many lifetime goals, I'd never be able to accomplish everything I desired if I checked out now. I wanted to see my little girl grow into a beautiful young woman. I hoped I had a book in me. Lying in that hospital bed, surrounded by pain, disability, and death, I discovered life.

I'd had an epiphany, affirming life and deciding to be nice to my body while recognizing my disability and its limitations. Choosing to like my body I began to like myself. I'd always perceived GD as an anchor weighing me down, preventing me from arising to my full capabilities. Lying in that hospital bed, I suddenly realized much of my life had also been enriched from experiences I'd had because of it. I embraced my life.

I had choices to make and I arrived at two important ones that day. First, I decided to stop being a victim, refusing to let my disease rule me. I'd become a person with a disability determined to walk my own path in reacting to the characteristics of my disease. Anyone, I realized, can opt to be a victim of anything—or choose not to be. I selected the latter.

Second, I chose to stop being bored. I could complain about

the tedium of life or I could relinquish that attitude. While spending weeks laying immobile in this hospital I'd managed to read, listen to music, watch sports, converse, and change my entire attitude about my life. I no longer needed to be victimized by boredom. I determined to return home a changed person.

Six weeks after arriving at Mass General my doctor asked if I was ready to move on. He explained I'd be measured for a back brace, a two-piece vest made of molded plastic. One side of the brace would cover my entire back, the other my torso, with Velcro straps connecting the two parts. Practice would be required for getting it on and moving around with it, since I had to wear it for at least six months. It could get wet, so I could even shower with it on.

With the fitted brace in place on my back, I moved into a regular hospital bed. I started physical therapy exercises and explored the hospital. Since I'd traveled east with a borrowed wheelchair, I navigated around the hospital when I wanted.

One day, someone told me another patient with my condition had been admitted. He couldn't leave his room, but I could visit. A couple years younger than me, he attended Harvard Law School. He lay immobilized with his leg in a cast, clearly in pain, with his girlfriend by his side. For the first time I'd met another person with GD.

Shortly thereafter my doctor informed me I'd be transferred from Mass General to a rehabilitation facility. That stopped me in my tracks. I balked. My physician looked perplexed, wanting to know the problem. Thousands of miles from home I didn't know anybody and everyone who mattered knew to find me at Mass General. If I left I wanted to return home, not to another Boston institution. My doctor incorrectly presumed I'd often been to rehabilitation facilities. I'd never even stepped into one. When he realized how upset moving into an unknown situation in a different location made me, he relented and offered as an alternative a week's stay on another hospital floor where a few people rehabilitated.

A week later, after learning rehabilitation techniques, like how to get up and down without putting undue pressure on my still weakened back, I arrived home in Oklahoma. Delighted to be there, though exhausted from months of pain and surgery, and tender and cautious in my movements, I chomped at the bit to return to my life—taking Aimée to school, going back to work, making love—but I wasn't ready to do any of those activities.

Then, a bombshell. Within days of my return, Gloria needed to talk. "I'm moving out. I've rented a place a few blocks away. Aimée will be nearby. I'll help you for awhile, get groceries and whatever else you need." More stunned than angry, I didn't argue. "Go" was all I could say. Even if I'd wanted, I didn't have the strength to fight.

Alone, focused on recovery, I screamed whenever I wanted and didn't bother anyone. I needed to regain my strength. To sleep, eat, and work. To become reacquainted with my four year-old daughter. To heal.

For the first time in years I found myself alone in my own space. I moved slowly. I looked at myself in the bathroom mirror. Even sitting in my wheelchair my height clearly had changed. When my vertebrae collapsed I'd lost about eight inches.

Within a few weeks I started to go into work. Probably too

soon for my physical, but not my mental, health. Driving home the few miles from our office at the end of the day my energy evaporated. Cooking wasn't an option so I patronized every fast-food restaurant between work and home.

After pulling into the garage and getting out of the car and into the house, I'd plop down on the couch in front of the TV to eat my fast-food dinner, not moving until bedtime, then following the same routine the next day.

I gradually recovered. One day I visited a new doctor who'd been recommended for his expertise with Harrington rods. He suggested in a few months he'd re-open my back and remove the top half of my rods. There was an element of logic to this because the tip of my left rod had started to cause pain. But another back surgery on my fragile bones? I didn't think so. I never saw him again. By the time I left his office I knew no one would ever get into my back again unless I couldn't move. The rods would stay.

It took about six months after returning from Boston to settle into new routines. Gloria and I divided the week as evenly as possible with Aimée staying with me three nights. We didn't split the time into blocks because we both wanted to interact with her throughout the week. We'd each pick Aimée up from school on our nights, but agreed to be flexible about our schedules.

By this time my energy crept to my norm. I slept without my back brace on, while wearing it during the day. About the time I got permission to stop wearing it completely my hematologist expressed concern about my parathyroid. Until that moment I didn't know such a thing as a parathyroid gland, which controls calcium levels in the blood, existed. As far as anyone knew only I, in the entire world, had both GD and hyperparathyroidism. An operation was planned to remove some of parathyroid glands, because we can't survive without all of them. Preparing for my third 1980s surgery, in the fourth year of the decade, I wondered how many more I'd need?

A couple months later, healed from my latest operation, I began moving without my wheelchair. Then I ditched my crutches and shortly thereafter my cane. I felt better than I had in years.

Chapter 10:

Walking Out, Sitting Down, and Moving On

To be effective a movement must be led by its constituents. People with disabilities are the only logical group to lead a disability rights movement. Only someone who daily lives with a disability can possibly comprehend its experience.
"The Walkout"

Back on the job, my thoughts returned to the contentious meeting about sheltered workshops on my first night at work. At that time I offered to investigate employment programs. A program called Projects with Industry (PWI), which was developed in many different ways around the country, impressed me because of its comparatively successful rate of finding employment for people with disabilities *and* keeping them in their jobs, which many other organizations failed to do. The ILP staff learned grant funds would be available to begin new PWI programs. Presenting this information to our Board, we recommended submitting a grant proposal. Not only did they nix the idea, but forbade us from spending any staff time working on this grant, stating we had enough other work to fill our time.

Unwilling to surrender, the ILP staff volunteered our time on nights and weekends and successfully submitted a grant application through the Norman Alliance of Citizens with Disabilities, a new volunteer organization we had helped create, composed of people with disabilities. It became the first consumer-controlled organization in the United States to operate a PWI.

We also declined to engage in the annual United Cerebral Palsy telethon. We believed telethons portrayed disabled citizens in a degrading and self-pitying way and refused to participate in them. We advocated developing public housing in individual dwellings, instead of high rises or the congregate housing UCP proposed, both examples we thought of as disability ghettos. We fought for—and eventually won—integrated (people with and without disabilities) one-story apartment complexes. We balked at streamlining our services to focus on the needs of twenty-four community residents, who had ties to the UCP-CC Board, at the expense of the hundreds and thousands of other citizens who needed our services. Finally, we demanded our Board be composed of a majority of knowledgeable disabled citizens.

UCP-CC, angered at our continued and persistent resistance to their dictates, restructured the ILP in early 1984, relieving Helen of her fiscal and administrative responsibilities—not firing her, but stripping her of all management oversight--and placing these responsibilities in the hands of a part-time UCP-CC Director, who hadn't been a part of the ILP and for whom we lacked respect because she seemed to us to have acquired her job for all the wrong reasons and none of the right ones. We fought these changes, submitting an alternate proposal that one Board member literally ripped apart. Another asked how we could possibly be effective employees when we had so much fun?

Flabbergasted, we listed our many accomplishments, including housing modifications; transportation advocacy; advising local merchants about accessibility and hospitality issues; and many modes of public education. On an individual basis, we'd taught many people with disabilities how to take care of themselves and advocate both for their own individual needs as well as more systemic ones.

The UCP-CC issued more dictums in response to our refusal to acquiesce quietly. ILP staff must use our time and equipment to answer UCP-CC phone calls in the absence of the part-time UCP-CC Director. This meant running to another office or programming calls into the ILP phone system. Helen protested these mandates, taking up the matter with independent living grant administrators in Dallas, who ruled such an answering service constituted improper use of grant funds. But the issue did not die. UCP-CC responded by making it clear Helen would no longer be permitted to make unauthorized long distance calls. In these days, when the telephone was still the primary mode of communication, this became a "straw that broke the camel's back."

One day in mid-April 1984, after addressing a group of elementary school children about disability issues, I returned to an empty office. I saw a message to meet my colleagues at one of their homes. After the latest order, making long distance phone calls essentially impermissible, we mutually agreed our only remaining course of action would be to walk out. We marched into our office, cleaned out our belongings, and left our jobs.

We didn't go quietly. We contacted folks at the building where we'd first officed, which housed many community organizations. The next day they donated office space. We called a friendly newspaper reporter. The local newspaper ran several articles about the conflict. We garnered support from disability rights advocates nationwide. One donated funds. A national independent living association investigated our complaints.

Acrimonious feelings ran rampant. We were accused of stealing ILP property. We sued for our final paychecks, including accrued leave. Clients venturing to the ILP were treated with uncustomary rudeness by temporary staff substitutes.

I wrote about our situation. A national disability magazine published "The Walkout." My individual job discrimination led to my personal radicalization, but the walkout taught me I'd joined a revolution. Parents, service providers, medical professionals, academics, and many others might have our best interests at heart, but until they listened to us, it didn't matter. We'd never obtain housing, transportation, jobs, insurance—equality—until we demanded it.

Despite support from our peers, we couldn't raise enough money to support us all and we began to look for other means of making a living. I began doing contract work. I scrounged enough money each month, month by month, to survive, supporting Aimée and myself. I learned another life lesson: I possessed survival skills not only outside the university environment, but beyond the everyday work world as well. I didn't know how I'd do it, but I believed I could get through unemployment.

My personal life officially changed as well. After a year of separation Gloria and I divorced, formalizing our makeshift custody arrangement.

In the fall of 1984, six months after the walkout, I obtained a new job as an ombudsman at our statewide disability advocacy office in Oklahoma City, about a twenty-mile, sixty-minute drive. A few weeks later my right knee imploded, ending the months of great health following my parathyroidectomy.

Balloon-like swelling mimicked a bone crisis. Like all previous bone crises, this one entailed intense pain, enormous swelling, and no weight bearing on my right leg. Staying home, I borrowed a wheelchair to get around. My new bosses were okay with my absence. They understood this sometimes came with the territory of my disability. They experienced less aggravation from the situation than me. I wondered why every time I started a new endeavor—school, work, marriage—my disability kicked in. I planned to wait it out—but it didn't end.

Finally I asked a friend to drive me to the University Hospital in Oklahoma City. The doctor who poked at my knee concluded this wasn't a bone crisis, but a knee injury reparable with arthroscopic surgery. I watched, stunned, when he opened my knee, stuck a tube in, and began sucking out fluid, blood, and bits of bone. He believed the pressure of accelerating and braking in rush hour traffic overstressed my knee and it responded with lots of little bone breaks. He recommended rest, keeping weight off my leg, and figuring out a way to drive to work that alleviated the trauma to my knee. I had one idea of how to do that.

A former accountant who used to work at the ILP had difficulty using an arm and a leg on one side of his body as a result of spasticity that occurred with cerebral palsy. To get in his car he'd installed a device called a chairtopper on the roof of his vehicle to transport his wheelchair without having to lift it himself.

I'd watched a few times, as he transferred from his wheelchair to the front seat. Once in, he folded his manual chair, and played with some switches on a small, freestanding metal box. The look-alike luggage rack on top of his car opened and a big hook on a chain descended. When the hook neared his wheelchair, he put it through the fold in the seat of his wheelchair, almost like hanging up a pair of pants, then went back to the switches inside his car, and the hook and chain reversed its direction and pulled the chair up and over, sliding it inside the box on top of his car.

I now needed to do this to transport a wheelchair without putting any weight on my vulnerable knee, or other potentially fragile body parts. I also needed to install hand controls, enabling me to accelerate and brake using my hands rather than my feet. The cost would be about $3,000. I didn't have that kind of cash.

I nervously ventured to my bank to see about acquiring a loan. I'd never done anything like this and when I explained to the banker what I wanted and why, he'd explained he'd never experienced such a request either and needed to confer with his boss. While I pondered what to do if this fell through he returned to let me know they'd decided to make the loan. Some people purchase clothes for a new job—I got a chairtopper.

The chairtopper and hand controls, along with a wheelchair, changed my life. I could now join family and friends, and especially Aimée, who'd recently turned six, at the mall, or the zoo, or concerts, or her school, without worrying my exhaustion or pain would cause the termination of these activities.

The chairtopper expanded my options. I could always have a wheelchair with me; but didn't always need to use it. I could walk and leave the wheelchair in the chairtopper, or unload it and push my chair to whatever event I attended or activity I pursued, depending on how my body felt at any particular time. I realized the time had come to purchase my own wheelchair.

When I parked in my garage, I usually left the chair in the chairtopper. That avoided the rigmarole of taking the chair out of the car and putting it back each time I arrived home and left the next day. I usually didn't need it.

I spent the next three years commuting to my Oklahoma City job. One beautiful spring Saturday I drove my car a couple blocks to a gas station to get a tune-up. While they worked on it I got into my chair, which had successfully relieved the pains in my hip, to enjoy a short walk home. The sun shone and I looked up toward the sky. The next thing I knew I lay sprawled on the ground, left arm under my body, wheelchair lying next to me. I'd rolled over a crevice in the sidewalk and my chair tumbled. In an effort to break my fall, I'd stuck my left arm out. I tried, without success, to get back into my chair. My arm hurt too much. Unsure what to do next I was saved from making a decision when a fireman stopped and helped me back into my chair.

I'd broken a bone in my shoulder and it needed to be immobilized for about six weeks. How would I get to work? I was unable to use my left arm to operate my hand controls or my right leg to work the pedals? I had no way to drive. Several frantic phone calls later I found someone who also worked in Oklahoma City willing to drive me.

Near the end of my third year at this job, I set my sights on working in Norman again. On each anniversary of the walkout I published a polemic about the continued lack of consumer control at the Independent Living Project. During that period, two Directors attempted spin-offs to consumer-controlled organizations and both failed. They tried to do this because UCP-CC knew the federal government would soon formalize consumer control into statutory language.

No appropriate organization existed in the collective UCP-CC mind to become the ILP's new sponsor, so they'd decided to create a new Board to govern the independent living grant. The first two attempts were the ones that had collapsed. I decided to apply for the position of Executive Director. After an interview with the same people from whom we walked out I was offered the job. Three years after the walkout we wondered if we'd won.

My tenure as Executive Director commenced in August 1987. A staff of unfamiliar faces guardedly awaited my arrival. A tentative Board watched to see if I brought hidden agendas.

Collaboration between the UCP-CC Board and myself resulted in the rapid approval of three Board members and an officially incorporated consumer controlled Board. Within a year the Board of Progressive Independence (PI), a name coined six months prior to my hire, grew to nine members. The official spin-off occurred on October 1, 1988. We had won.

While concentrating on developing the new organizational

structure, I'd lucked out with my Program Director, who'd been hired prior to my arrival. She loved providing direct services and facilitating their growth. Together we worked to expand the role of PI within the community and beyond. Two years after our hiring services and advocacy had expanded exponentially and our advocacy efforts became known nationwide.

As PI Executive Director, I attended the annual conference of the National Council on Independent Living, our national organization based in Washington, DC. Each year I tried to take at least one staff member who'd never been to such a conference. It was always an eye-opening experience, within and outside the conference. I'd make sure to wander around the streets of DC with my colleagues and each year they were amazed by the circuitous routes a wheelchair user had to take to get around the "accessible" city of DC. I often found myself in the middle of a street because of a lack of curb cuts or accessible sidewalks.

One year, two staff members and I joined a protest march called "Where is George?" In 1989, there was a push to pass a bill called the Americans with Disabilities Act or ADA. The first George Bush promised in his Presidential campaign he'd support the ADA, but once elected, he neglected that pledge. We gathered at the Capitol to march to the White House. Outside was a downpour, so March organizers passed garbage bags into the crowd to use as hats and umbrellas.

We left the Capitol, heading toward the White House, chanting, "Where is George?" We arrived at the gate fronting Pennsylvania Ave., a bedraggled, wet group, holding aloft candles in the rain.

After sitting in front of the White House gate for a fairly short time Presidential representatives contacted March leaders to schedule meetings to discuss support for the bill.

Despite our efforts, the ADA didn't pass in 1989. We again focused on getting it through in 1990. I'd become Chair of our regional Center on Independent Living (CIL) Directors (an association of all the Executive Directors in our five-state region), and in that position I regularly traveled to Washington to educate our legislators about the ADA. I sat in meetings with national disability policy leaders and learned about negotiating on the Hill, as part of a steady stream of advocates coming to Washington. When we first arrived we attended a meeting where we received assignments—specific legislators to talk with. I enjoyed wandering the halls of Congress and promoting the ADA. I met a couple of Congressional representatives, but mostly spoke with staff.

Back home, I'd taken a deep breath and submitted a proposal to facilitate a workshop at our national independent living conference. I'd begun exploring a concept called Disability Culture—people with disabilities creating our own culture—and wanted to test it out. Few conference organizers knew me so I figured simply handing in my proposal probably wouldn't get me too far. I approached two national disability leaders I'd met in the past few years to join me in a presentation.

One was Texan Justin Dart, well known in our part of the country. In DC now, he'd just resigned from a Presidential appointment over the same kind of issues that led to our walkout. He'd traveled the country collecting "discrimination diaries," stories of how people with disabilities had been oppressed over the years, planning to use these stories to help get the ADA passed. We'd met each other several times and I hoped he'd like my idea.

The other national leader I approached was Judy Heumann. She'd been a speaker at the first Oklahoma statewide independent living conference. Judy's parents, and then later Judy herself, who used a wheelchair as a result of contracting polio before she was two, fought the New York City school system. They'd refused Judy admittance to public school, classifying her wheelchair as a "fire hazard." She watched her parents win that battle when she was in fourth grade. Later, wanting to become a teacher herself, Judy encountered the same issue. Unlike me, she found a lawyer to advocate for her, winning a lawsuit against the school system, and becoming the first wheelchair user to teach in the New York public schools.

We'd communicated sporadically over the years since she first came to Oklahoma and I'd always had a good feeling about her so I took a chance and asked her to speak as well. I told Justin and Judy I wanted to create a session where we'd present personal stories for about half the workshop, then open the floor to the audience. I called the session, "Speakers of Movement: Voices of Independence." Both agreed to join me and the proposal was accepted.

At the workshop I talked about the walkout, now six years in the past, and unknown to many in attendance. Judy described summer camps, where she'd met and bonded with other kids with disabilities. Justin talked about the ADA. Then, as planned, we turned the remainder of the session, about half our time, over to the audience. Almost everyone raised their hands. Time vanished before many who wanted to speak had a chance. We left exhilarated, understanding we'd tapped into a deeply felt need to share our experiences.

I left Washington for Tulsa and a statewide independent living conference where I facilitated a panel called simply "Disability Culture." Did such a culture exist? If it did, was it beneficial? What characteristics comprised such a culture? How did it affect our lives? How might it impact nondisabled people? While no consensus emerged I'd found a subject to explore further.

During the same summer two other events changed my life. I traveled to Houston to attend a training for CIL Directors, and while sharing ups and downs of the job with peers I realized I'd lost my passion for my job, which had become too focused on personnel and bureaucracy and too little on advocacy. It was time for me to move on. Second, when I returned from a trip that summer Gloria showed up in my driveway with Aimée before I even got out of my car to go into my house. Looking into Aimée's face, I saw someone in despair at being shunted from one household to another with little control over her own destiny. I decided to change this situation to spare my daughter more pain.

I began a nationwide job search. While I knew I'd be devastated at being so far away from Aimée, I convinced myself it was for the best. I accepted a position as Training Director at the World Institute on Disability (WID) Research and Training Center on Public Policy in Independent Living in Oakland, California. Judy Heumann became my new boss.

Chapter 11:

Disability Culture and Pain, Plain

People with disabilities have forged a group identity.

We share a common history of oppression and a common bond of resilience. We generate art, music, literature, and other expressions of our lives and our culture, infused from our experience of disability.

Most importantly, we are proud of ourselves as people with disabilities. We claim our disabilities with pride as part of our identity.

We are who we are: people with disabilities.

"We Are Who We Are...So Who Are We?

Mainstream Magazine, 1996

Shades of brown and yellow in an unknown California bedroom caught my eye. Awaking in my Norman home little else from the dream remained—a glimpse of a woman's dresser and the initial "L" of a first name. Imagining names to fit the letter "L" only Linda came to mind, but I knew no Lindas in California, and in the San Francisco Bay area I knew only Judy.

Forgetting nighttime meanderings to focus on daytime realities, I looked into Aimée's eyes to tell her about my move, promising to see her often. During Christmas break she'd visit California. We waved goodbye in late October.

Pushing my manual chair along Berkeley's steep grades, near

the apartment where I'd rented a room, required more oomph than before and took an immediate toll in increased pain in my shoulders, knees, and hands, all of which I used to maneuver my wheelchair. I'd removed the footplates that came with my chair so I could move it with my feet whenever my shoulders or hands hurt.

At the World Institute on Disability (WID), I used someone else's office while I waited for mine to be ready. Her office mate showed me a picture of Lillian, the attractive woman at whose desk I sat, and her German boyfriend. I used her space while she traveled in Scandinavia.

Hanging out with Judy, being introduced to the many people who ventured into WID and others we worked with outside the office, led to meeting many activists I'd read about. One day Judy and I drove south to Stanford University, where she'd get a seating evaluation for a new wheelchair and I'd meet Paul Longmore, a historian with a disability whose work I admired and with whom I'd corresponded from Oklahoma. Sitting in one of his classes I learned about Jean Stewart's novel, *The Body's Memory*, the first fiction I'd read by and about a person with a disability describing experiences from a rights-oriented perspective.

Around the same time, someone at WID gifted me a ticket to a play called "Storm Reading," written by and starring Neil Marcus, a local man with a disability. He'd assembled the play from a collection of his anecdotes and imaginings, disparate writings, including diaries, newsletter pieces, and notes of various kinds. A wheelchair user who looked like he might have cerebral palsy, the audience learned his disability resulted from a condition called Dystonia. Neil performed the play, with both an American Sign Language and voice interpreter, since his own voice baffled many listeners. Watching Neil weave humor throughout the play, and after the performance, as the cast sat down to respond to audience questions and comments, energized me with experiencing Disability Culture in the flesh.

One Saturday evening, soon after seeing "Storm Reading," I sat in a line to see a local folksinger when I recognized Neil Marcus behind me. Introducing myself, I explained how his play fit into this idea I'd been toying with called Disability Culture. He responded with enthusiasm and we agreed to meet and talk and maybe even work together.

"Would you like some chocolate?" My back faced the door and I didn't recognize the voice. I turned to see a smiling woman leaning on a crutch with her left hand and holding a box of Finnish truffles with her right. Lillian, who'd returned from Sweden and Finland, walked through the office greeting old friends and meeting new people.

Within days, Judy invited me to Lillian's house to participate in a holiday baking party. We sat at a cozy table in her kitchen nook, playing with cookie dough. She again asked if I'd like some chocolate. "Yes, of course." Lillian then sent me over to a deep kitchen drawer loaded with more chocolate than I'd ever seen in one home, with bars from Japan, Germany, Sweden, and other exotic locations. Stunned at the array of riches, she came over and removed a huge block of Ghirardelli chocolate, slammed it against the counter, then offered me the half-foot piece she'd broken off.

In my quest to get to know people I asked colleagues to lunch or dinner. Lillian agreed to lunch. She immediately embraced the concept of Disability Culture, placing it into the context of her international work. Lillian observed no matter where she traveled or what types of cultures or social conditions she saw, individuals with disabilities always confronted oppression and she believed understanding the universal nature of disability resilience, as well as oppression, was the best way to move towards freedom. I enjoyed myself and hoped to get to know her better, especially after learning she broke up with her German boyfriend. I asked if she'd like to go out to dinner sometime. She ignored my invitation.

With the holiday season rapidly arriving I planned activities for Aimée's visit. Near my Berkeley apartment, we walked along Telegraph Ave., observing the many eccentric characters spreading their wares and pronouncements at all hours, and wandered around the Berkeley campus. I brought her into WID. In San Francisco we visited Fisherman's Wharf and FAO Schwarz, where Tom Hanks played the piano in the movie *Big*, and drove across the Golden Gate Bridge. Mostly we were together. The time quickly vanished and Aimée departed. We planned for her to spend a month with me during the summer. The pain of seeing her leave receded into work and a continued exploration of Disability Culture.

At WID one day, expounding about Disability Culture, responses from my colleagues stunned me. Individuals representing diverse genders, sexual orientations, cultures, ethnicities, and religions all resisted being classified as part of a Disability Culture, phrasing the objection as "I can't be part of a Disability Culture because I'm American."

Taken aback at first by this remark, I eventually got it: our society so denigrated people with disabilities that my colleagues, who fought fearlessly for gay, women's, and civil rights, among others, dreaded being pigeon-holed into one more stigmatized category, and as a result refused to identify with the most oppressed aspect of their identity. This conclusion persuaded me to work harder to develop a concept I believed could alleviate some of the stigma. I didn't yet know how it would happen, but my future work lay in the idea of Disability Culture.

In the meantime, a pressing task loomed before me—writing a brief explanation of independent living philosophy for an explanatory packet we wanted to distribute nationwide. Sitting in front of my computer during the Martin Luther King holiday weekend in 1991 to write the assigned two-page piece, I tapped page after page onto the computer. A month later, during the Presidents' Day holiday I stopped, having composed a monograph called "Independent Living: Theory and Practice."

Unveiling the unexpected 100-page document, my colleagues recommended sharing it with a few readers outside the organization to see what others thought. Some liked the theoretical chapters better than the practical ones, others reported the opposite opinion. In general, wider distribution was encouraged, but WID didn't know what to do with this ambivalent critique of the document I now called "ILTP," so we sat on it.

Approaching six months on the job in the spring of 1991, one of my bosses asked me to prove my mettle as Training Director, organizing and leading a staff training. I wanted to remove distractions by holding the training outside our offices, but the decision to stay in our less expensive space prevailed. Breaking that day for lunch, my co-workers headed to their offices, got on their phones or computers and started working. When the time came to reconvene, my colleagues remained immersed in their tasks. I hauled out my secret weapon: my "loud" voice, the one I'd used to address lecture halls of several hundred students without a microphone. Bellowing a summons to return to work, papers and phones dropped.

Later that day, I again asked Lillian to dinner and this time she agreed. We started out enjoying our conversation, learning we'd both recently left relationships and sharing how neither of us wanted to get married again; in fact, we weren't even certain we wanted future relationships. We began to describe our dream houses and learned they were exactly the same, in rustic settings amidst trees and alongside a stream. We both saw ourselves in our houses "living alone, even if we did end up getting involved with someone." By evening's end our dinner morphed into a date and we ended up driving elsewhere to cap off the meal and conversation with a dessert of ice cream.

A few weeks later, sitting across from one another in a Chinese restaurant I suavely lifted the teapot and asked Lil, "do you want some tea?" "Sure," she assented, holding out her cup. I proceeded to pour the tea all over her hand. She laughed it off, as I sat mortified.

Shortly thereafter, we went out again and discussed our spiritual beliefs. We'd each rebelled against the organized aspect of our religious upbringings and the tenets of our faiths. Lil attended Catholic schools, questioning religious doctrines at an early age, wondering "how a Peruvian saint who'd lived in abject poverty several centuries ago could have owned clothing that survived several hundred years to be sold as holy relics?" The nuns didn't like such questions and silenced her.

In the 1980s, Lil found a group of people who, like her, relied on their intuition to guide their paths through the world. They learned to channel an entity called Michael. Lil shared, "Michael consisted of a group of ascended souls who'd agreed to guide those of us still living on the physical plane." I asked "how I might learn more?" Lil breathed a sigh of relief, confessing she "didn't want to be in a relationship with someone who didn't respect her beliefs." This conversation began to re-awaken my psychic connections, buried since my unsettling freshman college experiences.

Within a month of our first date--where we declared we didn't know if we wanted another relationship, let alone live with someone else--I moved into Lil's house. Then, in the first few months we lived together I traveled to conferences in Washington, DC, North Carolina, and Illinois. In Chicago, my sister drove down from Madison. Walking along the lakeshore I shared my desire to create an organization focused on Disability Culture. We talked a bit about what that meant, then I put it on the backburner along with *ILTP*.

I returned to Oakland in mid-June. Lil and I planned to relax for a few days after she finished facilitating a workshop with a group of international disability leaders, and shortly before Aimée's July visit.

The night Lil's workshop ended we cuddled on the bed catching up when the phone rang. Almost as soon as she answered I sensed disaster. Lil's parents, vacationing in Canada, had been in a car accident when her Dad blacked out and turned into the path of an oncoming semi. Her Dad was in a hospital, but Lil's Mom died instantly.

Only beginning to learn the depths of Lil's story in the weeks we'd spent together, I knew her mother's loss would be devastating. Lil had a mysterious, undiagnosable disability, understood to be genetic because her mother experienced a milder version. They knew no one else with a similar condition.

Lil was born in Lima, Peru, her mother's home, in July 1951, a few months before my own birthday. She said she emerged "from the womb with both hips displaced from their sockets and hyper-elastic connective tissue." This super flexibility prevented doctors from realigning her hips because they "displaced each time they were re-set."

While Lil was a newborn, a friend of her mother's mentioned "Children's Hospital in Miami, Florida offered inexpensive medical care." After learning about this opportunity, her family first put Lil on a plane to Miami between the ages of eight to ten weeks. For months she traveled between Peru and Florida. At the age of one-and-a-half she went to this hospital for the final time. The doctors believed Lil suffered malnutrition and low calcium levels due to her many castings and immobilizations while they tried to rectify her condition. They decided to keep her in Miami.

Physicians believed Lil would fare better as a hospital resident, where they could perform surgeries at will. The family, unwilling to jeopardize Lil's medical care, didn't argue and at one-and-a-half years of age Lil began to live at the hospital.

When Lil was five-and-a-half her family decided to leave Lima for her father's home of Canada, so the two oldest children could attend better schools and learn English. On the way to British Columbia, Lil's mother, brother, and sister, none of whom Lil had seen since she was little more than a year old, picked her up from the hospital. When her family got her Lil spoke English in a Southern drawl, while her siblings spoke only Spanish. Lil was terrified. She didn't know these strangers who abducted her from the only family she knew—those at the hospital.

After two years in Canada, the family moved to the San Francisco Bay area joining two maternal aunts and seeking better paying job opportunities. Lil continued many hospitalizations, often at Shriner's Hospital, with more surgeries trying to improve her condition. By early adulthood she'd had about two dozen surgeries with more to come.

Shortly before I met Lil in late 1990 she'd experienced several knee and hip joint replacement surgeries. Needing time to recover in her Oakland home, her mother often drove over the Bay Bridge from San Francisco to help with groceries, cooking, and laundry. For the first time they discussed Lil's first few years. Lil wondered how her family could have abandoned her in Miami almost forty years in the past? She learned about the inexpensive medical care and other aspects of her early life she knew nothing about. Lil and her mother healed and strengthened their bond during this time and by the time I entered the scene they'd become close friends.

Weeks after beginning to date we joined Lil's parents, brother, sister, and aunts for dinner. I learned Lil's mom shared my love of Scrabble and baseball. We planned to get together during the summer and indulge both these passions, but before that happened Lil received the news about her mother's death. Lil left for Canada the next day to set her parents' affairs in order. She learned her father's blackout resulted from a blockage in his carotid artery and he'd need surgery after returning to California.

Days later, picking up my 12-year old daughter I explained why Lil wouldn't be waiting for us at home. Aimée digested the news as well as one might expect, anxious to know the new woman in my life. I wondered what kind of shape Lil would be in when she returned?

When Aimée arrived for her summer visit she'd yet to see Lil's house. In the six months since her last visit everything but my job was new. We walked up the ramp into a beautiful three bedroom 1920s house, with a large living room; dining room; kitchen; cat door, complete with cats; and a quaint breakfast nook. In the living room hung a tapestry Lil's ex-husband's grandmother created, a perfect rendition of the house and setting we'd described on our first date. Carved llamas and other knick-knacks and signs of Lil's Peruvian heritage filled the house. The downsides were only one bathroom and a basement where the washer and dryer stood beneath a flight of stairs. Lil had converted one bedroom into a den and rented out another, before I moved in and where Aimée now slept.

Lil returned from Canada a changed woman from the vibrant, engaging person who first attracted me. Taciturn and withdrawn, she tried to engage with the two of us while immersed in grief. As our month together drew to a close and we all faced a return to our "real" lives we regretted seeing Aimée going home to Norman to enter eighth grade, but figured it best under the circumstances.

Our focus on Lil's personal struggles receded for the moment into the background while we prepared for the oncoming autumn celebration of the twentieth anniversary of Berkeley's Center for Independent Living (CIL). At the conference I'd share my thinking about Disability Culture in a paper called "Creating a Disability Mythology." Facilitating a panel called "History and Mythology of Independent Living," with Paul Longmore and Neil Marcus, I'd decided to use mythology as a way to introduce my ideas about Disability Culture to the world, discussing the heroic journeys many of my friends and colleagues made in their lives. I declared, we must:

Embrace ourselves as we are with our disabilities,
our varied needs, and our diverse strengths and weaknesses.
To embrace ourselves as we know ourselves, with our
disabilities. I propose, in fact, even more. I wish to see us not
only recognize our disabilities, but to celebrate them. To sing
clearly and out loud our praises, our struggles, our failures,
and our successes: our lives.

When the panel finished, a man lying on a hospital bed asked if anyone living with a disability was a hero simply for being alive and going about their routine business. I responded:

> *Yes. Because of the oppression individuals with dis-*
> *abilities lived with in our society, I did believe we were all on*
> *a heroic journey. Just getting out of bed became a heroic act*
> *for some. Going to work for others. And here you are lying*
> *on a bed and attending a conference. Yes, I believe what lots*
> *of people call routine takes great effort on our part. It is he-*
> *roic.*

We may not match the escapades of a fictional hero like Huckleberry Finn, escaping confinement to travel downriver, harboring a fugitive, and setting out for parts unknown, but in our daily lives we confront social oppression, fight to move freely within a barrier-laden environment, and greet each day not knowing what adventures await us.

After the conference Lil and I didn't have much of a breather before we'd travel first to New England, a short return trip home, then leave again for Kentucky, Oklahoma, and Arkansas. I anticipated the latter trip for many reasons. I'd written a couple pieces I hoped would move me toward my next level in looking at life and disability and Disability Culture. We'd also visit Aimée and Lil would see my former home in Norman and meet my friends.

I'd hoped Lil and Gloria would get along, but that wish instantly dissolved when shortly before we traveled Gloria called saying "Aimée has become unmanageable, not listening to me, and refusing to go to school." Gloria said she "could no longer handle

Aimée and our daughter needs to live with you," moving to Oakland as soon as possible so she could start school in California in the following semester. Stunned, we didn't know what to make of this news and wondered who was this girl Gloria described, sounding so different than the Aimée we knew? We delayed making a final decision until talking in person with both Gloria and Aimée when we visited Oklahoma. After doing so, we agreed to Gloria's demand. We had no time to process how our lives would soon change because I got on another plane to work in Little Rock, while Lil stayed in Norman.

In Arkansas I delivered a speech called "I Was Born (In a Hospital Bed)—When I Was Thirty-One Years Old." I described being discriminated against in looking for a job, learning about the independent living movement, and lying in the Stryker bed, back broken, reliving my life-changing epiphany about appreciating my body. Concluding the formal paper, I breathed deeply and consciously set out to communicate Disability Culture through an example of the culture itself, with a just composed poem called "Tell Your Story," which began:

Tell your story

Tell your story

It may bump from the page

like words of Braille

sizzling in tales of blazing glory;

it may glisten in the sunshine like the Holy Grail,

so tell me a tale, even if it's gory,

*I'm yearning to hear **you***
*Tell **your** story.*

Applause rang out at the end of the poem and I left Arkansas triumphant. Reality soon set in upon returning to Norman. Lil and I discussed preparing our lives for Aimée to be in them on a daily basis. Lil decided she'd tackle the schools since she knew the area. I'd ready the house for Aimée's arrival and deal with the logistics of getting her to us. We had a plan.

In Oakland, Lil investigated the area's public schools, our first choice, but discovered no nearby schools afforded Aimée the type of environment or education we wanted for her introduction into her new life. Lil located a nearby private school that met all our criteria, except cost. In a meeting with school administrators we explained why Aimée would suddenly arrive in Oakland. Empathizing with our situation, and believing our background as individuals with disabilities could bring a needed diversity, they offered a scholarship. While still a financial hardship we agreed to Aimée attending this school.

An emphasis on drama at Aimée's new school appealed. We looked forward to seeing her in a play until we realized it would be held in a room someone using a wheelchair couldn't access. We talked with the school administrators. When they balked at moving the play I explained this new law, called the Americans with Disabilities Act required public events, such as this one, to be accessible to everyone. Changes were made and we saw Aimée perform and got a first-hand demonstration of the power of the ADA.

At work we all took a collective breath after the flurry of activities around the recently completed fall Conference and Lil and I exhaled our collective breaths from the extensive travel we'd just finished and the enormity of the change in our personal lives. I focused on sustaining the momentum built in the past few months, submitting my recent conference papers to two different journals. When both were published I thought I might achieve my dream of a career in writing and speaking.

After many conversations Lil and I decided to marry. We picked the next Valentine's Day because that came closest to when we first went out, we thought it'd be romantic, and it'd be an anniversary date we'd always remember. We discussed how we wanted a small wedding with only our closest friends and family. We started to make a list. Within fifteen minutes, we'd written seventy-five names. Laughing at ourselves, we threw out our list and started over.

Where would we want to have a wedding? Neither of us wanted to spend lots of money or make an enormous deal of a second wedding. We decided our house would be the perfect place. Then we let go of who would be there and thought more about what it would be like. We gave ourselves some time to contemplate it.

As the New Year came it was once again time to think about a wedding. We'd decided how we wanted to go about it. We'd hold the ceremony in our living room, in front of the fireplace. We invited our closest California friends, which meant three women, all single, whom Lil was closest with, and with all of whom I'd also become friends. Aimée would of course be there as well. The final member of the party would be the woman who married us, a lady Lil knew from her Michael channeling connections.

Seven people in all, including us, would be at the wedding. That meant lots of people who might want to be there, and whom we might want there wouldn't be invited, including my parents. We didn't share our plans with anyone from WID, because if we asked one person without telling more the small wedding wouldn't happen. We decided the best course of action was to keep our plans a secret from anyone not coming to the ceremony.

The day of the wedding it rained harder than it had for fifty years. Sheets of water cascaded onto the ground. Visibility was laughable—no one could inch outside without getting drenched.

Aimée, who routinely caught a bus home from school, couldn't see clearly through the pelting storm and boarded the wrong bus. When I walked into the house after leaving WID the phone rang. Aimée wanted to know if I'd pick her up at a gas station? She realized she'd been on a different bus when she got off in a neighborhood that wasn't ours. Knocking on several doors, no one answered, and she finally waved down a car. The driver she'd flagged offered to drive her home, but not wanting to lead a stranger to our house she asked him to leave her at a nearby gas station where she called me. With all of us now home and relieved Aimée was okay we praised her creativeness and clear thinking in a nightmarish situation. Then, we welcomed our small group of guests to witness us declare our love and commitment to one another with vows I'd written.

We gathered in our living room. We exchanged our vows and then wanted to celebrate. We'd planned on a steak dinner in downtown Oakland, but because of the frightening weather, we all decided to remain inside and order pizza.

A year later we invited everyone we knew to a reception, but one person was missing. Our world had turned upside down at the end of 1992, after Aimée returned to Oklahoma during her holiday break. On the date of her anticipated arrival back in Oakland we received a phone call from her mother--shortly after the take-off time of her plane--informing us Aimée would be staying in Norman because she no longer wanted to live with us. We were devastated and furious. There had been no warnings this might happen. It was one thing for Aimée to do this; she was a teenager without perhaps the best judgment, but another matter entirely for her mother to facilitate this action. Before I knew it I picked up the phone, leaving a stern message telling Aimée "to get her butt on that plane or forget she had a father." I couldn't believe those words came out of my mouth, but it was too late to retrieve them.

Aimée wrote us saying she was afraid if she returned to California we'd never let her go back to her mother again. We'd discussed Aimée's staying with us through high school, but not seeing her mother again? Where did these thoughts come from? Lost, we sifted through items left in her bedroom. Some writings we found there made no more sense to us than her note. Not knowing what else to do we called the therapist she'd been seeing. Aimée had discussed this move with her, but in California if a client 12 or over didn't want the therapist to reveal anything they couldn't approach anyone about it. When it became clear Aimée wouldn't return, she wrote her therapist giving her permission to speak with us. Her therapist shared with us some conversations they'd had and encouraged us to see a therapist ourselves, not to make sense of what could only be described as an illogical situation, but to work through our grief and anger.

Not wanting to take this lying down any more than when I'd been told I couldn't write a book, I called a lawyer who informed us California law permitted a child Aimée's age to determine with which parent they lived. I could fight it in court, but I'd likely lose and what might that do to an already fractured relationship?

Nothing prepared me for this turn of events. How could my little girl reject me? What had we done? What had I done? I was angry, but even more confused. What could possibly have led my "daddy's girl" to so completely shun me? Heartbroken, I had no way to make sense of her actions. I didn't know what to do with myself or my feelings of abandonment and loss.

Helpless, I joined Lillian one day when she went to see her therapist, who explained adolescents often played one parent against another, but when divorce entered the picture it was like the child had a nuclear weapon to use against each parent—choosing with which one they'd live. Without legal recourse, we did the only thing we could—talked with friends who'd had similar experiences. They all said there's nothing to do but wait, somehow let Aimée know we loved her, and hope when she turned eighteen things would change. Their experiences demonstrated this happened more often than not as soon as the child officially reached adulthood.

We decided we'd send birthday and holiday cards and wait. What else could we do?

One thing we did do was sit down and make a list. We both

knew about tests where people listed major life stressors and how they often led to some kind of illness or other deleterious effect on someone's life. Thinking about our time together we started with my move into Lil's house right after Lil had some minor surgery. This continued on with her mother's death, her father's surgery to repair his carotid artery, being informed Aimée needed to live with us, getting married, and Aimée leaving. We'd drawn up about ten times as many situations as the experts said led to illness and sometimes death. Finishing this task we put our list down and tried to move on.

The next fall, Lil left for about six weeks of work in Scandinavia. After each trip abroad, she'd become increasingly dissatisfied with the Bay Area's intensifying gridlock and booming population. I'd never been enamored of the Bay Area as a place to live. I loved the people at WID, and liked the work, but had a difficult time with middle management. I still wondered if the independent living monograph I'd written should see the light of day, but I knew it wouldn't happen at WID. Ready to move on, professionally and geographically, Lil and I decided to look for somewhere else to reside.

We'd actually started to think about moving when Aimée lived with us but hadn't gone beyond talk. Now we were determined to find some place with a climate better suited to our bodies and a lifestyle better matched to our temperaments. We laid out some criteria. Since painful arthritic symptoms were secondary aspects of both our disabilities we sought warm, dry weather. Both of us were convinced the humid, foggy Bay Area weather accelerated our pain. We also thought a slower pace of life would benefit us both. We felt a need to be close to the professional and social opportunities a university offered. Our final criterion was to live no further than an hour away from an airport because we foresaw more travel. We also had the luxury of owning, free and clear, a house in the Bay Area and knowing even in an economic downturn we'd be able to live almost anywhere. The population of Las Cruces, New Mexico, where I'd lived in the mid-1970s, had grown to about 60,000, and fit all our criteria. Since Lil had never traveled to this part of the country, and I'd not returned to Las Cruces since 1976, we chose to spend our summer 1993 vacation there.

We arrived in Las Cruces on a late June night with me anticipating Lil's introduction to the jagged precipices of the Organ Mountains, an exquisite site, especially when refracting multiple shades of light at all angles. Lil was not impressed, noticing the lack of vegetation, so unlike her verdant northern California mountains. Hoping she'd change her outlook we wandered around for a day or so and Lil began to appreciate the desert's subtle beauty. We drove up to Truth or Consequences and west to Deming and Lordsburg to explore the state on our way to visit my parents, who'd relocated to Tucson when they'd retired.

By the time we returned to Oakland we'd made up our minds. We'd put our house on the market and move to Las Cruces. There we'd start the Institute on Disability Culture as a not-for-profit organization we hoped would support us. I'd applied for a fellowship to research Disability Culture and if that came through we'd have a year's income as we built the Institute. I submitted my resignation at WID.

Upon leaving WID I dredged out "Independent Living: Theory and Practice," printed ten copies and let some friends and colleagues know I had a monograph for sale. Several sold immediately, enhancing my self-esteem and encouraging me to keep putting my work forth into the world.

I also kept writing poetry. One day I composed "Pain, Plain," unexpectedly beginning:

Pain, I went to write the words
But before I could put finger to key
I was caught by the sharp, intense
and, oh so familiar, pain in my knee.

Concluding, "No matter how fancy the wrapping/The pain remains plain with plenty of trappings," I decided to keep writing about pain and, if ever presented the opportunity, to talk about it as well.

We sold our Oakland house, found one we loved in Las Cruces and chose to move during the long Thanksgiving weekend in November 1993. We'd drive to Tucson to celebrate the holiday there before continuing the drive east to our new home.

A year later, we drove west to Tucson for another celebratory Thanksgiving weekend. The fellowship had come through, the first federal funding to support research about Disability Culture, and we'd created the Institute on Disability Culture. Halfway through our first New Mexico year we bought a guest book to document the social magnet our Las Cruces house had become, counting about 100 houseguests, including my parents, friends from California, Lil's relatives, friends from Europe, and new friends we'd met since moving to New Mexico—and we'd traveled about half that year.

We'd returned to California for my Disability Culture research and to visit friends and family. We spoke about independent living philosophy at conferences in Washington, DC and New Orleans. In Denver, we made a foray into exploring Disability Culture, but attracted only a tiny audience at a diversity conference where most of the attendees didn't perceive disability issues as their own. In Las Cruces, we'd had chances to discuss Disability Culture with wider audiences, but the majority of our work led us to the El Paso Airport, 56 miles from our driveway.

Toward the end of the year, as my fellowship concluded, I wondered how I'd apply my research. The funding agency required a report with few parameters, so I wrote "Investigating a Culture of Disability: Final Report," which became an Institute monograph. Observing in it, "The next grand paradigm change in disability has already happened. It is the Disability Culture Movement" I anticipated promoting the concept as widely as possible in the coming years.

Professional successes belied intensifying physical pain. Despite Las Cruces's warm, dry climate, my pain worsened and I'd increased my daily intake of narcotic painkillers. I decided to learn more about Enzyme Replacement Therapy (ERT) for Gaucher, described in a long-ignored letter received just after moving to California, from my Oklahoma hematologist. Physicians had developed a synthesized form of the enzyme missing in those of us with GD. The drug, called Ceredase®, was culled from human placental tissue and had been injected into individuals with GD to alleviate, and in some cases reverse, the disease process.

Upon getting the letter in Oakland, I chose not to pursue ERT for several reasons, including concern about side effects and data sharing ERT's lessened impact when people's primary symptoms were skeletal. Enzymes could not be taken orally and therefore had to be injected, entailing trips to a hospital several times a month for infusions. This didn't enthuse me either. But while preparing to deliver a Disability Culture presentation in Oregon in 1994, I experienced a bone crisis for the first time in many years. I had no clue why it showed up now. Although Lil had heard me describe bone crises, she'd never seen me in this kind of pain. I didn't know if I'd be able to make the trip. In the midst of this agony spewed "In Need of Comedy:"

Attacks, we used to call
them. Before bone crises
became the fashion.
I describe myself with medical
words—enzymes, metabolic, lipids—
bone crises of my youth.
I write poems and essays about pain;
I speak and train
about my people.
Earn respect with my tongue,
a pen, what exists

above the shoulders.

Today,

none of it matters.

I cannot move

without a scream.

Lay my ankle

against the sheet,

cry out in agony.

Turn sideways

caught   suddenly

shockingly

immovably

by a

suffocating

wave

of

pain.

Disturbing my wife

scaring the cats

remembering

long ago.

Invaded by a screaming, bayonet-wielding, poison-dart, dag-
ger-tipped unending militia. Attacked is how I feel.

The bone crisis faded and the trip to Oregon happened. But the experience led me to revisit the idea of ERT treatment. When I did my life changed in the most unexpected ways.

Part II: Healing

It is only with the heart that one can see rightly.
What is essential is invisible to the eye.

Antoine de Saint-Exupéry

Chapter 12:

Travels, Rocks, and Bones

We are all individuals; we are all members of multitudes of groups. Each of us is full of change, compromise, and various abilities—and then we change again.

Aviam Soifer

When we lived in California Lil introduced me to Otto, a German friend. After we moved to New Mexico, Otto called saying he wanted to explore the Southwest. He became a regular visitor during our first year in Las Cruces.

Lil first met Otto when he led a group of German visitors with disabilities to Berkeley for a six-week training she conducted. They realized they had much in common, including a mutual interest in exploring metaphysics.

A Physical Therapist who wanted to expand his treatment methods, Otto learned modalities including Cranial-Sacral Therapy and Visceral Manipulation, both involving gentle, hands-on healing. Talking with Otto about his work spurred me to explore alternative, or complementary, healing methods. He cringed when he witnessed my pain and asked why I didn't take advantage of the synthesized enzyme treatment we told him had been developed for GD. I gave my standard answer that "it just didn't feel right and it seemed it had been pushed through awfully fast."

Despite pain, travel highlighted our lives after we moved to

New Mexico. In fall 1995, building on Lil's extensive overseas work, we visited Sweden, working in Gothenburg and then taking the train to see friends in Stockholm. Starting the journey, so excited I could hardly stand it, I slept for only an hour or two between flights from El Paso to Houston to Zurich to Gothenburg. On the longest leg of the trip I marveled at Ireland's beauty during sunrise.

I looked forward to setting foot on European ground when we landed in Zurich, Switzerland. With time before our next plane left for Sweden we planned to explore the Zurich airport and rest a bit, but surprises awaited. The first shock was the ease of deplaning. Waiting, as always, for everyone else to exit while our wheelchairs were retrieved from the plane's belly, we were unsure how we'd get down, since we weren't at a Jetway. We didn't need to fret. A machine similar to the one that delivered food to the planes rolled toward us carrying our wheelchairs. After the driver parked the machine adjacent to the plane, a platform hoisting our chairs rose to the door. We exited the plane, sat in our wheelchairs and were lowered to the ground on this machine, then headed toward the airport entrance—and our next, less pleasant, revelation.

Wheeling off to explore the airport we suddenly found ourselves confronted by two stern women in Red Cross uniforms who explained their instructions to take us to the airport hospital while we awaited our next flight. Almost, but not quite speechless, we insisted we didn't need to do any such thing—and didn't intend to. After a brief conversation, in which our resistance became clear, the nurses decided we must sign a release saying we refused this "medical" treatment and assumed full responsibility for whatever might happen to us while we wandered about on our own in the airport. We did and then went on our merry way seeing the few sights to be viewed in the surrounding areas, then entered a pleasant lounge where others with lengthy layovers also awaited their flights.

Landing in Sweden, Lil's friends met us at the airport and drove us to the apartment where we'd stay. It had a nice kitchenette with a refrigerator they'd stocked.

Queen of jet lag, Lil suggested sleeping a couple of hours, then getting up to adjust to the new time zone. That sounded reasonable and we drifted off. Two hours later the alarm rang and I jumped up ready to begin the next phase of our trip. Lil looked daggers at me and wondered why I bothered her. Reminding her of her plan, she quickly dismissed me saying she needed sleep. I asked if she wanted me to make her some food? She glared. I left her alone.

We had a great time both working at the independent living center in Gothenburg and seeing our friends and historic Stockholm. We began our return trip routed through Amsterdam instead of Zurich. There we again requested gate checks for our chairs to Houston, just as we had in Gothenburg for Amsterdam. This meant that our chairs would arrive at the door of the plane on the Jetway, rather than in baggage or at the gate waiting area or somewhere else where we wouldn't be able to easily access them. The Amsterdam airport personnel wanted to check our chairs straight through to the El Paso Airport. For once, I instantly became more insistently stubborn than Lil, refusing to let them tag our chairs. Who knew how we'd get around the Houston airport during our layover there if we didn't have our chairs—our legs—waiting for us.

The standstill came to a head when gate agents readied passengers to board the plane. They wanted us to go through the gate's security first and get on board. Normally, that's just what we'd want to do too, so we could settle on the plane before others bounced by us. But since our chairs had yet to be tagged—to go anywhere—we refused. At this point Lil and I sat about twenty feet apart. A gate agent looked at Lil and asked her to persuade me to let them tag our chairs through to El Paso and then get on the plane. Lil shrugged her shoulders. She couldn't do anything with me any more than could they. We'd reached an impasse with my refusal to move until they tagged our chairs to Houston. Knowing one possibility was we wouldn't get on this plane, I held firm. Luckily, they decided they'd rather be rid of us than face whatever might happen if we missed our plane and tagged our chairs to Houston.

A downside of manual wheelchair use is the toll it takes on shoulders. Navigating long passageways, sometimes in a nerve-wracking hurry to get from one gate or terminal to another to catch flights, aggravates tender joints and bones. During this trip our shoulders ached as we powered our way through airports. At home, exhausted, each of our pains accelerated. We decided the time had come to acquire motorized wheelchairs. I'd avoided this as long as possible because non-folding, several hundred pound wheelchairs also meant a van with either a lift or a ramp to load them into. The cost of such a vehicle ranged in the neighborhood of $30,000 to $40,000.

Researching New Mexico's Vocational Rehabilitation (VR) agency policy we learned they were one of the few states still paying for and modifying vans. I made an appointment.

When I arrived the counselor told me they only worked with people seeking employment, not with ones already working. Informing her she was mistaken and offering to show her where in the VR manual post-employment services existed, she realized she knew less than me and backed down. We proceeded to work together to get a van.

While I worked on getting a vehicle, Lil contacted our insurance company to start the process of obtaining motorized wheelchairs. We soon found ourselves sitting in our new motorized wheelchairs but with nowhere to go beyond our neighborhood. This lasted several months until we obtained a full-sized van with a lift. The van sat so high off the ground I had to use my chair to get in and out. I stopped walking outside the home and at home I began using my new motorized chair most of the time because walking now hurt so much.

A research protocol into Gaucher Disease (GD) caught my attention. The National Institutes of Health (NIH) and Massachusetts General Hospital scientists sought participants just like me. Someone under the age of forty-five who had experienced severe bone pain, undergone a splenectomy, and never used Enzyme Replacement Therapy (ERT). Nearing the cut-off age I applied. I figured to at least receive a baseline report on my overall GD health.

To determine suitability for the protocol required a series of tests at NIH and my old haunt of Mass General in Boston. The results shocked everyone. Even with NIH's and Mass General's sophisticated machines my bone density could not be measured. This petrified me. How did I move at all if my bones were so weak and fragile? The doctors urged me to get on ERT without delay.

We contacted Genzyme, the company that manufactured Ceredase®, the synthesized ERT drug, and they sent a representative from Houston to our New Mexico house. The salesman wondered "Why would you wait so long to do this?" He couldn't fathom someone with my history ignoring this obvious solution to GD, especially since Genzyme ensured everyone who needed the drug got it. Ceredase® was then the market's most expensive prescription so cost became a real issue and I asked "why Genzyme would be so willing to make sure I got it?" I never got a convincing response about the company's apparent altruism.

After the salesman left I still harbored intuitive doubts about using the drug, but had no practical reasons not to take it. I could imagine no other way to feel better. Lil abhorred witnessing my pain and if something could alleviate it she wanted to give it a go.

Ceredase® (which in later years became replaced with Cerezyme®, which doesn't use human placentas) mimicked glucocerebrosidase to stimulate elimination of the fat cells that accumulate in someone with GD. Getting ERT becomes a life-long commitment because the body discharges the synthesized enzyme within a couple of weeks. Optimal ERT treatment had been established at two week intervals, with the amount of the drug given intravenously based on the recipient's weight. Since I'd first heard about ERT infusions had moved from hospitals only to a variety of settings, including homes and places of employment.

After finally choosing to use the drug everyone insisted my

first ERT treatment needed to be at my doctor's office in case of an adverse or allergic reaction. My physician was also uncommonly nervous about administering the precious medication and didn't want anything to spoil the treatment.

This first experience didn't endear me to the process. My doctor tended to be disorganized. She planned to close her office to all other patients that day to focus solely on me, but an emergency occurred and I ended up waiting as usual. Otto happened to be visiting during this time and he accompanied me to my first ERT treatment. He couldn't believe the inefficiency.

By the time my physician was ready both our nerves made it hard to find my usually visible veins. It took five tries of sticking the needle in me before getting started. Once the infusion finally began everything else proceeded smoothly. Otto recommended meditating during my infusions to assist the ERT to be as effective as possible and I tried to do so. I began a schedule of every other week ERT treatments.

Since GD is metabolic in origin many of us had experienced an inability to gain weight no matter how much we ate. Even when my vertebrae collapsed and my 6'4" inch frame shrunk to 5'8", I maintained my weight of about 150 to 160 pounds. This hadn't changed since my mid-twenties. Gaining weight might signal the ERT had an effect.

During my first six months on ERT I didn't put on any weight, but did notice increased energy. Unfortunately, my pain also exacerbated. Inquiring how this could happen someone suggested since ERT changed the bone structure in the process of alleviating the disease perhaps increased pain resulted from the process of my bones adapting.

Six months later my weight changed as I quickly put on twenty pounds, but the pain didn't abate and my improved energy leveled off. I still questioned ERT's efficacy, but without an alternative I continued the infusions.

Otto called one day to say he had a new girlfriend and they wanted to visit. He brought Eva to us and Lil found a new sister. Walking around our house Eva noticed rocks in our many nooks and crannies. Lil had started collecting rocks as a girl but I'd never paid them much attention. When Lil told Otto and Eva she'd discovered a compelling local rock shop they planned to check it out. I stayed home.

They returned several hours later at dusk. Otto and Eva both smoked, but since we didn't permit smoking in our house, they moved to our back porch to light up and sift through their acquisitions. To be sociable, I joined them.

Removing the rocks from their boxes they started passing them around. Each of us held them. Now dark and unable to see the rocks well, I surprised myself by feeling their energy and announcing to a startled trio: "this one is about humor," or "this one is about healing," or "this one is about joy." I had no idea where these comments originated, but they kept coming. Some of the rocks emitted so much power my hand burned. Without understanding what was happening, I eagerly anticipated the next rock I'd caress.

Lil owned several books about the energies of rocks and wanted to see if the authors confirmed my pronouncements. Melody's *Love is in the Earth* series catalogued and described rocks from the perspective of the author who is both a geologist and meta-physician. To our astonishment the statements I'd made about the energy of the rocks matched Melody's analysis. We then looked in a second book, based on information received from Michael, the entity Lil channels, and again found agreement with my statements. Feeling like I'd been hit in the head with a rock, I started joining Lil on her forays to the rock shop.

Lil had yet to invite me to sit in on a channeling session, but if I bumped into her clients they made sure to tell me how much Lil's sessions meant to them. Connecting to stones precipitated a change in my internal life and I began to wonder when I'd actually see Lil channel. Before that occurred, a call from one of Lil's god-daughters late in 1996 sparked a demonstration of my internal evolution.

Living in Juneau, Alaska where her family ran a bed-and-breakfast, Gwen, Lil's youngest goddaughter, planned to marry in December and wanted Lil at the wedding. Lil thanked her but said there was no way her body could travel to Alaska in mid-winter. A week later Gwen called back and asked would a May wedding work? Lil, deeply touched by the change, said we'd be there. Hearing the news, I commented we hadn't taken a vacation since moving to New Mexico, so why don't we spend a month in Alaska? Lil gazed at me like my senses had vanished, asking "How could we possibly afford that?"

I had a contact in Alaska who'd expressed interest in us doing some work with his agency. I emailed him to see if May might be a good time and let him know why I asked. Then we recalled a woman who lived in Anchorage and offered to host us if we ever made it there.

While trying to figure out how we could make this trip happen we visited the rock shop. Another customer and I spied a particular rock at the same time. We removed it from the glass case. A combination of quartz, smoky quartz and citrine, the other person remarked this unusual confluence of minerals represented prosperity. Thinking about getting to Alaska, I bought the stone and placed it in our bedroom.

A day or so later my Alaska contact called saying he had a gig for us about a month before the wedding. They'd pay for travel, lodging, and a speakers' fee. Our vacation became a reality.

In Anchorage, we rented a car that didn't have the hand controls I needed so Lil did all the driving, and after completing our work we traveled around the area. We preceded the midnight sun by a couple of months, but it remained light late into the night, perfectly fitting both our natural body rhythms. Getting up in the morning and eating breakfast I'd enjoy the beginning of the day, while Lil slept. When she awoke, plenty of daylight hours remained.

If Lil tired she'd pull off to the side of the road and nap and I'd read, take a short walk or just sit still. Leaning back one day with the sun beating through the windshield I sat quietly, meditatively, and found myself connecting with an unknown but enticing energy that seemed to be talking to me. Was this Michael? I didn't know, but sensed the energy giving me a message that if I applied myself I might channel too. When I mentioned this to Lil she concurred. I stocked the information in my memory banks.

We'd taken our manual instead of our motorized wheelchairs on our trip to Alaska to ease the process of flying and car rentals. After returning to New Mexico, we became painfully aware our bodies didn't recuperate as quickly as they used to. Between our chronic pain and what had evolved into chronic fatigue we no longer could count on our bodies to sustain us to travel and work as we'd been doing since moving to the southwest. We needed to make a decision about how we'd survive. Acknowledging how much our disabilities now limited our ability to work we applied for Social Security Disability Insurance (SSDI), which had been established in recognition that disabling conditions sometimes prevented people from working typical forty-hour weeks. A recipient, though, could do a restricted amount of work within specific guidelines.

The great limitation of SSDI is the amount of income most people derive from it. A complicated system, based on the number of quarters one's worked and paid into Social Security during a specific period prior to applying, neither of us would receive much money on SSDI. But if we could survive, SSDI gave a gift of time, which I planned to use to read, write, and study new subjects, including my awakening curiosity about metaphysics. Before that happened, I found myself in unexpected, uncharted territory.

Chapter 13:

Time to Heal

Our duty, as men and women, is to proceed as if limits
to our ability do not exist. We are collaborators in creation.
Pierre Teilhard de Chardin

Disability Culture remained the guiding force throughout my work, despite the lack of a steady paycheck to pursue it. When first sharing my Disability Culture poems at the beginning of the 1990s I hadn't read much poetry myself and had never been trained in the art. I had difficulty perceiving myself as a poet but I realized my poems about the disability experience resonated with many of my peers. "Tell Your Story," began to be requested and led to my developing confidence in sharing new work. Writing poetry became part of my daily life.

My central theme that people with disabilities are fine just the way we are drove my research and writing. A new poem, "Sonata in the Lingering Keys of Life" included:

The greatest compliment you could once bestow:
"You don't seem any different to me"—
In my eyes you are normal—
meaning you are like me
somersaulted into an insult
while you weren't looking.

What makes you,

white man, black man,

red woman, yellow woman,

brown child, rainbow race,

Believe that putting two feet on the ground,

Waving two arms in the air,

Having a face unmarred except caked,

Thinking in a straight line

Or famed, artistic, eccentric convolution

Spells normality,

Meaning if you are not like me

You had better want to be like me...

Normalized?

"Normal" had become a dirty word within the disability rights movement. What did it mean? Who was normal? Someone who could move on two feet, see, hear, talk, think, and work like the average, middle-aged adult? That excluded millions of people in the U.S. alone, including Lil and me. Thrilled to express such thoughts in poetry as well as prose, my writing continued in this vein, while various forms of art became a more significant part of my world.

I'd recently purchased a handheld Native American drum and discovered a local group that offered lessons, the New World Drummers. African drums called djembes and djun djuns were strewn about the room when I rolled into class one Saturday morning. While most participants used djembes, single drums coming up to the knees from the floor and played with both hands, I wanted to play my Native American drum that could be hit with a stick. Otherwise, my hands would take a beating, I'd be in pain and unable to continue drumming. Explaining my reasoning led to being welcomed as a member of the group. Leaving two hours later I anticipated the next class and became a regular weekly attendee.

A year later, the drum class moved to the Court Youth Center, an arts center named after the street on which the building stood. An introduction to the Director of the building stimulated a conversation about physical access. This talk facilitated varied experiences, including meeting many local artists. One woman ran the literary Border Book Festival. We spoke about incorporating access and individuals with disabilities into the annual spring Festival. I also became involved in teaching community writing classes and took a playwriting class with local legend and author of *Children of a Lesser God*, Mark Medoff.

I became a guest poet at a high school, then a poet-in-residence at local middle schools, and a Women's Shelter. Teaching poetry to an after-school group of pre-schoolers and kindergarteners who hadn't yet learned to read stimulated me to suggest creating picture poems. Loving being in the midst of this writing world, a poem called "What Do You Do When Your Dreams Come True?" described my feelings: "They called me a poet/I didn't know what to do/What do you do when your dreams come true?"

About the same time, another dream materialized. As our friends predicted, when Aimée turned eighteen in 1996 we renewed our relationship. We sent a birthday gift that year as we'd been doing since we lost contact with her four years before. For the first time since she'd left California she responded. We began a tentative correspondence and started talking on the phone. Before long she said she wanted to visit. It would be another year before that happened, and we used that time to get to know each other in letters and on the phone, while moving on with all our lives.

In the fall of 1997, Lil and I traveled to Germany to visit Otto and Eva and attend their wedding. Eva had honored Lil by asking her to be a witness. Before that day, Otto and Eva hosted a social gathering at their home one night, and introduced us to Knut and Ulrike, a physician and his wife who described alleviating pain as their passion and life mission. They described investigating different treatment modalities before settling on one called Pulsed Signal Therapy, or PST®.

When someone is born their cellular structure is designed in a certain way. The idea behind PST® is as our lives progress various traumas create pain in the cells around ligaments and tendons and change their cellular structure. PST® machines contain an air-coil system resembling a ring sending out electro-magnetic signals to stimulate the body to rearrange cells to their original non-pain situations. Invented by a researcher at Yale University, but still controversial in the U.S., PST® mimics the body's natural signals in activating the healing process. It's believed to decrease pain and increase functional capacity with any joint or musculoskeletal disorder.

Knut generously offered Lillian and me PST® treatments. He thought his chances slim of ever again meeting individuals with our medical histories and he wanted to know if it could help. We jumped at the chance. It totally changed our trip because we'd need two treatments a day to accommodate the short time we'd be in Munich. Each treatment needed to be a certain number of hours apart and we had to have at least one day in between two blocks of treatments. We now committed most of the time we'd be in Germany to getting the treatments, but Otto and Eva supported anything that might help us feel better, and friends we'd just met offered to transport us and ensure we obtained the treatments.

When we first arrived at Knut's office we encountered an elderly lady. She told us before she started PST® she'd needed shots just to get out of bed in the morning and enable her to do any activity. After the PST® she felt like going dancing. We eagerly entered the office.

Knut suggested we utilize the PST® machines on areas of pain we most wanted to ease. I chose my lower back, which had ached since my surgery over ten years before and seemed to be where much of my pain had settled. Lil asked for work on her hips. Since both these treatments required lying down I brought a book and read through the first treatments. After a few sessions, I noticed Lil laying quietly. Asking why, she replied she meditated. That sounded like a good idea so I followed her example.

After several PST® treatments, my lower back hurt less than it had in years. Lying on the table one day toward the end of our series of treatments, Ulrike came in to say hello and ask how we were doing. Without much thought, I remarked "I think I need to focus on healing. I've written and talked about pain enough. It's time to move to healing." Not knowing what these words coming out of my mouth meant, I realized they felt right and needed me to pay attention.

Despite our many trips to the PST® machines, Otto and Eva's wedding was the reason we'd crossed the ocean and we celebrated their wedding at a small country church near Munich. In our manual wheelchairs, which we still used to travel to Europe, we sat at one end of a long table during the wedding reception, held at a nearby lake. Opposite us sat a tall, broad man, with straight blond hair flowing to his shoulders, who resembled the Marvel comic book character, Thor. As people finished eating he walked toward us. Introducing himself as Herwig and trying to help us pronounce his Germanic name, he turned to Lil.

"Excuse me, may I ask you something?"

"Okay" she replied.

"Are you clairvoyant?" Herwig inquired.

"Well," Lillian stammered, "I'm a channel."

They spoke a bit about this, then the three of us conversed a little. Herwig and Lil decided they wanted to meet again in a few days in a quieter setting and we invited him to come to Otto and Eva's apartment. Before departing, Herwig spoke to Lil once more, "Excuse me, but I feel I have to ask, does your left hip bother you?"

"Yes!" Lillian replied.

"It's from before you were born," Herwig stated.

He didn't mean while she lay in the womb. He meant from another lifetime. Lil forgot this exchange for a long time, but it struck me like a thunderclap.

When we next met Herwig, he explained he too was a healer. In fact, he and I had briefly met. I'd ventured to Otto's office one day, choosing to suffer the pain of ascending numerous steps to see where he worked. After climbing once I knew that would be my only visit. That day Herwig had come in and worked on Otto, but I'd paid more attention to my book than to the two of them.

We learned Herwig met Otto and Eva attending a course on Cranial-Sacral Therapy. When doing homework for this class Herwig started seeing things he couldn't decipher. Asking his teachers about his visions, they responded they didn't understand either and advised he further explore the information coming to him. Doing just that, Herwig, who'd been trained in both physics and homeopathy, began a healing practice using concepts of energy. He still sought words to translate this inner sight, especially in English, but said his healing work focused on what he called the "energy body."

At that same meal, Herwig explained he acquired his excellent English from his father, who taught it in German schools, and while he'd wanted to visit the U.S. he had yet to do so. Describing our large New Mexico house we welcomed him to visit anytime. Saying he might do that, he said his goodbyes, leaving us with much to ponder.

Not long afterwards, Germany receded below us as we flew back to the States. We left with much to think about and looked forward to soon seeing Otto and Eva and a group of Germans who'd join them in another wedding at nearby White Sands National Monument.

Chapter 14:

Miracles

There are only two ways to live your life.
One is as though nothing is a miracle.
The other is as though everything is a miracle.
Albert Einstein

We began entertaining German friends arriving for Otto and Eva's U.S. wedding--the one they'd always considered their "true" marriage ceremony. The four of us shared a love for the magic of White Sands National Monument. Ninety minutes northeast of Las Cruces, a few fenced-in dunes separated the Monument from the highway, masking the enchantment within.

The drive into the Monument led to a shape-shifting world of drifting sands, light-skinned lizards, and hearty plants. The further one traveled into the dunes the more moon-like the landscape became, with the white sands reflecting the sunlight against a backdrop of mountains.

For Otto and Eva, White Sands provided a perfect spiritual ambiance—and they invited all their friends to witness their American nuptials. Every corner of our house filled with overseas visitors. Lil helped locate a Native American shaman to perform the ceremony. On our way there we spotted a double rainbow and sensed the universe blessing this event. When we arrived at the parking space near one of the Monument's pull-away drives, we immersed ourselves in the energy all around us.

Sitting in a circle, surrounded by guests in ceremonial dress and musical instruments all around, the shaman asked Lil and me if we wanted to renew our vows on this night as well. Only married five years, we thought what the heck, here we were, yes we'd do that. After the ceremony, the shaman told us we'd been visited by two Native American elder spirits who stood behind us, hands on our shoulders, as we re-committed to one another. We'd felt their presence.

Lingering a bit beyond the Monument's closing time, a Ranger arrived to urge us to end the festivities, but when he learned of the Native American rites being conducted he suggested we remain as long as needed. We eventually drove toward home filled with hope and wonder at the night's events.

The next morning most of our visitors left to explore other parts of the country, planning to return at various times in the coming weeks. But Lil's sister and two friends from the east coast remained. Our lives continued to fill with friendship, savory kitchen aromas, and incandescent conversation.

Since returning from Germany my reading and exploration in various metaphysical fields continued. We'd become friends with a woman who combined her Native American and Hispanic backgrounds into her own unique healing style. She introduced Lil to a curandera, a Hispanic healer. Something vague yet real lurked beyond the physical but I remained on the brink, struggling to cross this precipice.

My announcement about healing to Ulrike while I lay receiving the PST® treatment led to retrieving the multi-volume *A Course in Miracles (ACIM)* Eva and Otto had gifted me. *ACIM*, a channeled, self-study teaching curriculum of metaphysical thought, is designed to provide an intentional, healthy approach to inner peace and unconditional love.

The *Course* resulted from an unasked for and unexpected voice entering the mind of an Eastern U.S. university professor. Try as she would, she couldn't shut it out. Fearing she was losing her mind she sought a colleague's solace and advice. He asked her what she heard. When she explained the information the voice conveyed, her colleague suggested they record the voice. They spent several years doing just that without asking whose voice they transcribed. Then one day they found the courage to inquire about the entity's identity and the voice replied Jesus. The professor didn't appreciate the irony of a Jew—even a non-practicing one, who described herself as atheistic—channeling the voice of the Christian savior.

The spirit of Jesus recognized this dilemma. A conglomeration of many souls, it suggested she think of the entity like an elder brother offering wisdom. Since the first publication of *ACIM* in the mid-1970s, A Course in Miracles classes formed all over the world. Several existed in Las Cruces and we now offered to host one at our house. As we immersed ourselves in the teachings, the Course resonated more with me than with Lil. While Lil drifted away from the Course, I read all the books, including a workbook of daily exercises, which I practiced.

Before Lil left the Course she'd made a lasting contribution, suggesting one night we call the entity EBJ (Elder Brother Jesus).

We all checked in with the entity and the term seemed to fit so we continued using it.

While throwing myself into learning *ACIM* and connecting with the entity we now called EBJ, it appeared the time had arrived for me to practice channeling. At first, many voices or entities crowded into my consciousness, making it difficult to focus on one message. To resolve the confusion I concentrated on listening to the consistently available voice of EBJ.

Each morning I'd start the day with a meditation and channeling EBJ. Eventually direction came to transcribe the information received, in poetic form, leading to publication of *Journey Home: A Miracles Poetry, Prayer, and Meditation Workbook.*

Before that happened, though, confidence in my ability as a channel needed boosting. Alexandra, who facilitated our *ACIM* group, also wanted to improve her channeling, and we agreed to support one another in the process.

One day, while we practiced with each other, I asked a question about a persistent issue—confusion over my using a wheelchair. Ambivalence about using a wheelchair didn't come from within, but for reasons beyond my understanding my wheelchair use had become a bone of contention for other people. Some told me they saw me using a wheelchair for the remainder of my life; others informed me they saw me walking. Not foreseeing a day when I'd abandon my wheelchair, I wondered why this statement so often recurred and why others felt compelled to share their notions about it with me.

When asking the entity about this conflict, Alexandra voiced the response as something like, "as long as you've chosen to communicate in this way this lifetime, that is what you'll do." That cinched it. Moving through life using a wheelchair made sense. Having a disability and using a chair led to my life's work. The Universe intended me to navigate the world on wheels.

Chapter 15:

Re-connecting

We all carry the knowledge for perfect well-being within us.

This knowledge is contained in our energy body.

Herwig Schoen

In the midst of my spiritual growth spurt we boarded a plane for Germany and Hungary. Using Otto and Eva's Munich apartment as our base for our six-weeks stay, we'd work in Munich, at two Centers for Independent Living in northern Germany, and speak at a conference in Hungary. Lil would offer individual channeling sessions and a group channeling session in Munich.

Thrilled to travel to Budapest and see a new country we boarded our plane. We stayed in that city one night, then traveled by train from Hungary's capitol to Gyor for the Conference at which we'd speak. There we participated in the nascent disability rights movement's first street demonstration, protesting the many inaccessible downtown buildings. We also met an old friend of Lil's who'd been born in Hungary, but now lived in Munich. She drove to the Conference and offered to give us a ride back to Germany. I jumped at the chance to see more countryside, while Lil chose the quicker flight. Enjoying every second of the ride, I especially loved the short break in Vienna where we toured the home of the avant-garde Austrian architect Hundertwasser.

Together again in Germany, Lil and I soon boarded another

train for Mainz and Kassel where we'd work with disability groups, then return to Otto and Eva's. Once back in Munich, our focus turned toward Lil's channeling and socializing. Our friend Maria, who we'd met on our first trip and with whom I'd established an instant connection, demonstrated a healing method called "Metamorphic Technique," a gentle massage of the hands, feet, and head, or spinal reflexes, designed to break old patterns and then hopefully leading to transformations. Explaining my sensitivity to touch didn't deter Maria who insisted it wouldn't hurt. I gave it a try and found it so soothing I wanted to learn more about it. Perhaps a change did occur. During Lil's channeling I unexpectedly participated.

Lil sat in Otto and Eva's dining room channeling Michael during the day while our friends were at work. Closed glass doors separated the area where Lil channeled from the hallway and bedroom, where I lay behind another shut door. Despite these barricades, the channeling seemed to hurl itself into my space. Images of rocks whose energy would be meaningful for the person receiving the channeling persisted so strongly they compelled me to listen for the conclusion of the session, then shout out the name of a stone. Surprised, Lil wondered why I entered her channeling space, but when the information matched hers, she began to anticipate my contribution. This happened so many times that when Lil later facilitated a group channeling, I co-channeled with her, specifically offering suggestions for rocks useful to someone's life.

We also renewed our acquaintance with Herwig, who asked many questions about my disability and Enzyme Replacement Therapy (ERT). On this lengthy trip I'd brought several vials of ERT with me for infusions at Knut's office. They were stored in Otto and Eva's refrigerator. Removing one I handed it to Herwig.

Assessing the small bottle for a few seconds, Herwig declared, "This is poison." Without equivocating, he said his statement didn't indict ERT in general or its efficacy for anyone else. In my case though Herwig strongly believed ERT not only did not help me, but had a harmful impact. While stronger than my own intuition about the medicine, Herwig's comments fit too closely to my own sentiments to dismiss them but I wasn't yet ready to give up on ERT; I had nothing with which to replace it.

Herwig decided the time had come to travel to the U.S. He arranged his trip and would travel to New Mexico before we returned from Germany. That was okay with us, and he left for the States to stay at our house while we remained in Europe.

The Course in Miracles class continued meeting at our house during our travels and we told Herwig he'd meet like-minded people there. That turned out to be a great steppingstone for him and when we arrived in Las Cruces Herwig introduced us to new friends.

Within a month of our return, Lil and I were scheduled to speak at a Wellness Conference in Farmington, in the northwestern corner of the state. Deciding we wanted to do something fun we'd planned to offer a relaxation workshop. Herwig would speak there as well. We all thought this would be a good opportunity for him to introduce his ideas.

The conference would signify Herwig's first public speech about his work. Already nervous, it became more unsettling because he'd not interacted with a group of people with disabilities. He wanted to test his ideas on Lillian. They decided to go to a juice store where they could sit outside in the sun and talk privately. I tagged along. While we sipped on our drinks Herwig shared his thoughts. He'd recently come up with a name for his work: Reconnective Therapy (RCT).

He conveyed we each possessed an energy body as well as our physical body. While these two bodies were distinct aspects of ourselves, they weren't separate. Our physical body mirrors our energy body. The energy body is not a manifestation of our mind, but a distinct entity, which some people see quite clearly, as others see auras, and still others see eye color.

Herwig believed dis-ease and dis-function existed because of a dis-connect between our energy and physical bodies. He thought it possible to work on re-forming this dis-connect.

He insisted we must release our notions of time and space and remember we are all connected to one another. When we divested ourselves of our temporal, and temporary, attachments our essence remained. When he practiced RCT he connected energetically to the one constant of the universe, love. From there he could connect with someone else's energy body and facilitate reconnections leading to healing. In fact, he described himself as something like an electrician rerouting wires, but in his case he reconnected information between someone's energetic and physical bodies. He concluded stating his belief anyone could do this work.

While we didn't understand all Herwig's words, he moved us both with his impassioned sharing of his knowledge and beliefs. My intrigue level soared, wanting to know more. Asking questions about what he did led Herwig to offer to treat me.

At home, he asked me to lie on our six-foot long, oak, dining room table. Surprisingly it felt good to lay there. Sturdy enough to hold me easily, high enough for me to get on and for Herwig to bend toward my body, I awaited his approach. How would this work? Herwig explained he'd gently touch me while connecting with my energy body, then become quiet for a few minutes while he worked, and when complete he'd let me know what happened. Closing his eyes, he released a breath and looked like he'd disappeared into the universe. I shut my eyes, too, trying to imagine the process. Herwig's breathing changed, marking his return to his body—Lil's phrase describing when she came out of a channeling. To no one's surprise he stated the treatment had been on my bone structure. While he saw lots of weakness in my bones he also believed RCT could help. But he insisted my ERT infusions harmed me. From his talk outside the juice store, inklings of what he meant began to penetrate into my consciousness.

ERT might positively impact the physical manifestations of my Gaucher Disease (GD), but it interfered with the desired connection between my physical and energy bodies. Herwig, in facilitating re-connections within my energy body, believed the ERT blocked the desired re-connections my energy body wanted to make with my physical body. Furthermore, he believed my body intended me to have GD—the disease wasn't a mistake, or a curse, or even a bad thing. GD caused me all kinds of pain and suffering, but came into my life for a reason. Perhaps I'd be better off attempting to live with GD, not trying to eradicate it. ERT sought to temporarily replace my malfunctioning enzyme, all it could do; but maybe Herwig and RCT offered a different, non-invasive, longer-term solution. Perhaps focusing on repairing the energetic dis-connections stimulated by the disease would lead to a re-connection between my physical and energetic bodies in areas where GD led to dis-ease, pain, and broken bones.

Herwig treated me a few more times before we all left for the Wellness Conference in Farmington. Anxious about his first experience around a crowd of individuals with disabilities, Herwig set off by himself for the Wellness Conference in northwestern New Mexico. He'd arrive before we would so he could join a group of hearty souls who'd kayak a nearby river. Amazed and energized by his experience with a joyful and daring group of people with disabilities he got an inkling of why we didn't see ourselves as victims of our conditions.

By the time we got to the Conference, we found Herwig engaged in animated conversations. His eagerness to interact with others led to a well-attended session.

Emotional in preparing to deliver his message, Herwig asked Lil to sit with him while he shared his thoughts with the audience. Describing energy work, and for the first time using the term "Reconnective Therapy" in public, the information resonated with some and bothered others who wondered, if Herwig, like many medical doctors in our experiences, discounted living with a disability and wanted to cure us of our ailments.

This tension between what any healer—traditional or alternative—offered and our quest to live as people with disabilities, struck

at the core of our beliefs. We'd worked for decades to convince society those of us with disabilities lived meaningful, productive, and
proud lives despite existing in a society filled with prejudice and discrimination based on disability. A core principle that we didn't need
to change, society did, informed all our thinking. Now this man Lil
and I brought to the Conference claimed we didn't need to hang onto
to our disabilities if we didn't want to. How could we merge this
kind of thought with being proud of who we were as people with
disabilities? That question had to be addressed. But before that happened Lil and I had our own workshop to do.

We sat in a circle with a group made up primarily of rehabilitation counselors and social workers who bemoaned missing relaxation in their lives, especially while working. We'd brought along
many toys to help them. We passed a basketful of stuffed animals
around the room urging everyone to take one. Lil cajoled even the
most reluctant men to hold one. We'd brought rocks, musical instruments, and wind-up toys. Essentially, we gave everyone permission to play and they loved it. When the session ended we again
passed the basket to collect our toys and stuffed animals. A few attendees didn't want to relinquish "their" possessions. We urged them
to find their own toys.

At the end of the Conference, Herwig, Lil, and I drove about
15 miles northeast to spend a couple of days with friends in Aztec.
He planned to travel through a bit of the southwest before returning
to Las Cruces, and then back home to Germany, which gave me time
to think about next steps.

Never having achieved comfort with ERT now I sought confirmation of Herwig's analysis of the drug from our metaphysical circle. Each responded in the same way, though not as dramatically as Herwig. ERT didn't help or hurt me. All believed other solutions lay before me. Clueless about what might actually happen, I leapt over the precipice.

When Herwig returned to the U.S. six months later we came to an agreement. I'd stop using ERT while he treated me regularly, which for the foreseeable future meant on a weekly basis. A mammoth decision, which almost no one thought I'd made correctly. My doctors didn't. My family didn't. Lillian didn't know but tried to be supportive.

My home health nurse surprised me with her reaction. She'd been injecting me with ERT for a couple of years and when we talked during the hours she spent at our home I learned of her background in both Western and alternative healing work. Many times we'd discussed my feelings about ERT and mostly she listened. When I'd made up my mind to stop ERT she let me know she admired my determination to listen to my heart and follow my intuition. Coming from someone in the medical profession this helped me believe in my decision.

Herwig began treating me when he returned to the U.S. late in 1998. He used our house as a base for the next six months. One day, thinking about how RCT worked, we talked about whether a treatment needed to be in-person. Herwig described energy work as being outside the realm of time and space and into a different reality. Just as radio or television frequencies travel around the globe, so too does our energy. When a practitioner is connected to the energy of the Universe, he or she can locate the energy of the person they're treating. Two conditions that precede this connection are an agreement between the practitioner and the person he or she is treating giving the practitioner permission to do the work and the practitioner's intention to do the best treatment she or he can do. That's how he connected with another's energy body. So did he have to be in the same space as the person he worked on? I didn't see why. He thought about it. In the meantime, he described seeing improvement in my bone structure, but I didn't feel much different. My pain remained.

Herwig left to visit other parts of the country, and we planned our trip to Tucson as we did each November to celebrate Thanksgiving with my parents. This year we'd also spend the weekend after the holiday with friends in Phoenix.

In the hours before our trip we realized our van modifications needed immediate repair. We detoured east to the closest repair shop, in El Paso, for an emergency fix. On our way an enormous pothole couldn't be avoided. Our van bounced off the ground jolting us. Lillian yelped on impact, but recovered quickly. Steadying the van back onto the road, the shock dissipated from my body, and we drove on to the shop, got the van repaired, and headed west.

During the couple of hundred miles through the mountains to my parents' house my left hip began to ache, the pain increasing with each mile. By the time we arrived, moving my hip at all proved difficult, let alone putting any weight on it. Unable to walk and throbbing with pain, no one wanted to be around me much—including me. Gritting my teeth to get through Thanksgiving didn't thrill me, but no alternatives materialized.

Maybe leaving my parents' home and keeping our date with our friends in Phoenix would relax my body and lessen the pain. But as we pulled into the hotel parking lot the necessity of a Herculean effort to exit the van dawned. Summoning each ounce of reserve, I emerged from our vehicle, made my way into the room, flopped onto the bed, and didn't know when I'd next be able to move.

Disappointed but knowing we'd be unable to leave the hotel for our Friday dinner with our friends we called to inform them of my status. They kindly brought food to our hotel room.

It finally occurred to one of us (probably Lil) to call Herwig and ask him to treat me. Believing RCT could be practiced long distance but not having experienced it, I wondered what he'd be able to do. Herwig connected with me energetically and said he didn't think there was a crack in my hip, but if I wasn't careful it could happen. He recommended remaining off the hip for the immediate future. He wanted me to call him the next day for another treatment. After a couple days, leaving the hotel room--with great effort--became possible. Continuing to stay in touch with Herwig we waited for him to signal it was okay for me to make the ride home, with Lil driving and being as gentle as possible on the highway.

During the next week or so, Herwig treated me several times. Within a month, with no traditional medical intervention, my hip felt normal. For the first time I internalized how effective RCT could be. I intended to learn this technique.

Chapter 16:

Anger

Holding on to anger is like grasping
a hot coal with the intent
of throwing it at someone else;
you are the one who gets burned.
Buddha

During one of his explorations around the country, Herwig set out for California. Before he left, we'd talked about two people we thought he'd want to meet: Lil's brother and sister, who both still resided in the San Francisco Bay Area. Herwig planned to stay with Lil's brother and his partner, who also had a welcoming house.

Keeping in contact with Herwig during his travels we quickly learned Lil's sister and Herwig meshed. The situation with Bill, Lil's brother, became convoluted.

While Lil's brother had been a juvenile-onset diabetic, no one in her family, with the exception of Lil, considered him to have a disability. Still, Bill, who'd had many problems with his eyes as a result of his diabetes, investigated alternative healing, even studying with the Dalai Lama in India. Always living on society's edge, he'd also learned and practiced Chinese and Tibetan medicine.

In the 1990s, Bill discovered he had testicular cancer. After having one testicle removed, he explored treating cancer with alternative methods. He found an herbal oncologist and together they developed a protocol for treating his cancer. Using this protocol, Bill remained cancer-free for the next five years.

Bill and Herwig shared a common way of looking at the world beyond the non-physical perspective, but they also each possessed a tinge of arrogance about their own practices that prevented them from becoming the best of friends. To complicate matters, Bill and his partner, Alice, had ended their relationship, but Bill still lived in Alice's house and Herwig and Alice were attracted to one another. We'd spent a little time at Alice's house during a visit to San Francisco and we knew we'd want to stay friends no matter what ended up happening between her and these two men.

Returning to Germany once more Herwig injured himself in a motorcycle accident. Alice traveled to Europe to be with him. After leaving the hospital they returned to California for a period of recovery.

As Alice's kids became young adults, neither she nor Herwig wanted to stay in California. They decided to move to Santa Fe. We were excited about this, thinking we'd get to see them more often, even though we rarely ventured that far north. An old friend of Lil's, José, who'd been in the same Michael channeling group she'd attended in California, now lived in Santa Fe. Lil talked with him periodically and now she told him about Herwig and suggested the two meet. José helped them find a house near his own.

Herwig wanted to offer RCT classes in New Mexico after obtaining a work visa. Introductory in nature they were intended for anyone interested in learning about this new healing paradigm. He wanted to offer one class in Las Cruces. We suggested hosting the class at our house and Lil agreed to help find participants.

While Herwig and I had become closer since first meeting, the relationship between he and Lil had become strained. Much of the tension occurred when he lived with us and continually neglected our access needs. Forgetting to move chairs out of the way of our wheelchairs or leaving messes in the kitchen for us to clean up frustrated us. We needed to maintain our house a certain way so we could move easily within it.

We had a plastic lawn chair Herwig used when he sat at one of our computers. We'd converted one of our bedrooms into Lil's office and another into mine. One day I rolled into my office and found the lawn chair sitting in front of my computer. A painful effort was required for me to move it, necessitating getting up from my chair to put it somewhere else. This day I'd had it. So I moved the chair into the middle of Herwig's bed. When he returned I'd left the house, so his response was to ask Lil if I was okay. Flabbergasted, Lil wondered why that was his reaction? But he stopped leaving the chair in front of the computer.

While petty, this incident was neither isolated nor confined to Lil and me. Others had similar experiences. Herwig's penchant for picking up a piece of fruit and pronouncing it inedible had become legendary in our little circle, for he not only made the announcement, but then went even further and threw out the offending food—whether it belonged to him or someone else.

Amidst these tensions, Lil and Herwig's relationship deteriorated, but so did some others he'd developed since coming to the

U.S. With this backdrop, the class began.

About half a dozen of us sat around our living room listening to Herwig introduce himself and his work. When he'd begun his healing practice in Germany, he'd owned a successful tree-trimming business. An affinity for trees enabled Herwig to communicate with them, explaining why trimming needed to happen and how he and his crew would go about it. He also discussed his undergraduate degree in physics and his training as a homeopath, but didn't dwell on these past aspects of his life, preferring to get to RCT.

He described energy work, and how it differed from allopathic, or conventional, healing techniques that treated symptoms based on physiology. Traditional healers, like many Western doctors, separated physical symptoms from any other aspect of our existence, such as spirituality—or energy. Focused on what we can learn through our five senses modern medicine appeared grounded in the scientific method, even though no one understands how the most common of remedies—Aspirin—works.

As Westerners, trained to believe in science and what we learn through our senses, energy work defies our common understanding of how the world functions. Because we can't see energy with our eyes we needed demonstrations. A large part of this five-day introductory class focused on conveying what we knew without being able to see with our eyes.

One day Herwig asked us all to close our eyes, then placed an object in each of our hands. Keeping our eyes shut we described what we held. Although all the objects were ours, I couldn't figure out what rested in my hands, but sensed love emanating from it. I described this feeling and Herwig affirmed my sense of the object. When I opened my eyes I recognized a small, wooden turtle.

The point of the exercise had been to demonstrate we "knew" more than we could "see." We all possessed an ability to connect to inanimate objects because, like everything in the universe, they too are composed of energy. When we connected to this energy we sensed the properties of each object.

Herwig worked on each of us as part of the class. We all observed, hopefully with our mind's eye, his treatments of us. And others not in the class, but who wanted to be treated, also showed up at our door, and we watched Herwig work with them as well.

Many times, while working on someone, Herwig described various parts of our anatomy. This proved to be a difficult part of the class for me. Herwig believed we all needed to have a basic knowledge of anatomy to understand RCT. But I found myself drifting off whenever the subject arose. Maybe because of all the times I'd ignored doctors in my life, I found myself unable to focus. I knew I needed to learn anatomy, but I didn't know how I'd accomplish that.

From the beginning of class, Herwig referred to two processes called brain stem activation and "initiation." With brain stem activation a connection is made between an individual and what Herwig called the first energetic frequency. With initiation an energetic connection is made with the second frequency. Each of these connections enables someone doing this work to connect with different aspects of energy and facilitate working with this technique.

Herwig told us on the first day an "initiation might happen in our class." He'd check at the end of class and if someone was ready he'd facilitate the process. Our bodies would facilitate the connection whenever we were ready. He'd tell us on our last day of class if anyone had been initiated. Although he didn't intend to make us feel like we'd failed if this didn't happen, many of us believed that's what he meant. (Since the time of this class, he no longer does this, because initiations now happen with treatments whenever a person is ready.)

When Herwig announced only Alice, his girlfriend, had been initiated, this led to increased suspicion about the process. Rancor and dissension ruled the class by this time and many were ready to leave before Herwig wanted to dismiss us.

Herwig insisted he needed to speak with each of us individually before we disbanded. He wanted us to know how he'd assessed our progress. Herwig surprised me when he said I'd be unable to immerse myself in RCT work until I released my anger. I thought I'd done a decent job of doing exactly that over the years. I certainly didn't feel as angry as I once had. Hadn't I gotten rid of my anger lying in the Boston hospital bed?

The more I contemplated his words the more I saw their validity. I remained angry about lots of things—discrimination against people with disabilities—my people; how I'd been unfairly treated because of my own disability; why did I still have to live with intense pain; how hard it had been to work within this society as an individual who didn't fit into the "norm" of social expectations; how little the government supported those of us with disabilities; how poorly the town we lived in treated individuals with disabilities; how difficult it was to sustain the lifestyle we wished to live; and so on.

An endless list formed.

Later, when I had a chance to continue this conversation with Herwig, I recall him declaring "the type of anger I held could lead to depression--often defined as anger turned inward"—which he believed was directed at God. "Until I could forgive God for the way my life had turned out, I'd be unable to benefit fully from what RCT offered."

Wondering how to respond to Herwig's assessment inspired me to return to meditation to release anger. Years before, attempting meditation, I'd invariably fall asleep. Mentioning this to someone they asked "What's wrong with that? Lots of people envy anyone who can relax so completely and that in itself is a kind of meditation." On hearing this reaction and receiving permission to meditate in this way, my preconceptions evaporated.

But most of the time I still couldn't meditate in a way that seemed meaningful to me, so I sought assistance. Researching meditation and stones led to the discovery that Kyanite held energetic properties that facilitated meditation. A trip to the rock store and purchasing a small piece of Kyanite worked well, so well within a few weeks I no longer needed the stone to enter concentrated, wakeful meditations.

Experimenting in diverse environments and situations proved instructive. Meditating while waiting to see a doctor led to my lowest blood pressure reading since turning 40. Perhaps some anger did dissolve. I decided to meditate an hour a day and see if it changed my life.

Chapter 17:

Walking

In order to be a realist you must believe in miracles.

H. C. Bailey

My internal drive to achieve didn't disappear when I got on Social Security Disability Insurance (SSDI). No longer able, or desirous, of working full-time, each morning I'd arise, fix a cup of iced coffee, and wheel to my computer. Not having to report for a job didn't mean not working.

We'd inherited a little money, which inspired me to learn rudimentary aspects of how the stock market operated. Wondering if materials I'd written over the years might be published in book form led to reviewing and compiling my essays. After a few hours, as morning moved into afternoon, lunch beckoned. Reading while eating preceded my daily meditation. Later in the day, I might continue reading, watch sports, practice drumming, run errands, or teach poetry.

We decreased our traveling because of our increasing pain. Not wanting to confront the horror and enormous energy required for two wheelchair users to get on and off airplanes and make airport connections, the distances we covered decreased. We still loved the desert, but missed water and greenery.

Lil poured her time into improving accessibility within the city, but the never-ending, frustrating battles extracted a physical and emotional toll. We began to wonder if it might be time to move. But if so, where would we go?

Standing in a grocery store checkout line one day my back suddenly shook uncontrollably with a searing, paralyzing pain. Unable to move, as the pain snaked its way throughout my body, I feared I'd be unable to pay for my groceries or even make it back to my car. But before I could do anything the pain subsided enough for me to move again. Still, I couldn't fathom what could cause that kind of literally breathtaking pain. Gingerly leaving the store my mind filled with fears of a second back surgery.

Before contacting my orthopedic doctor I called Herwig, who reported a hook on the left side of my spine had detached from my Harrington rod. He believed my body no longer needed the hook to be connected to the bone. Happy to hear this opinion, I still wanted medical confirmation. An X-ray showed the hook resting loose in my back, which my physician recommended leaving alone unless it caused me any problems. I also relayed this information to doctors in the east who knew my Gaucher story. They also advised leaving it alone. This confirmation of Herwig's statement convinced me more than ever of the value of Reconnective Therapy (RCT) and of Herwig's readings.

One day about this time, Lillian's older goddaughter, now living in Sacramento, phoned with news of her wedding. Like her sister, she wanted Lil there. If we'd travel to California anyway, why not vacation as part of the trip, as we'd done in Alaska?

Upon turning 40 I'd set two goals for the next decade: learning to fly and visiting Hawai'i. Having given up on flying as my body deteriorated, the thought of the wedding heralding our way across the ocean appealed.

I'd guessed my attraction to the islands occurred when they became a state in the late 1950s. Lil had vacationed on both O'ahu and Maui in the early 1980s, before we'd met. She'd even declined a job offer in Honolulu, not wanting to leave her mainland family, friends, and support systems. It didn't take arm-twisting for her to return to Hawai'i. This opportunity sounded perfect.

We knew a couple people in Honolulu. One, in particular, a former professor we'd met at disability studies conferences, moved to Honolulu after he retired from a Boston university. We let him know we'd be coming and hoped to see him, but decided we didn't want to make this a disability rights trip. We wanted a real vacation, not combining work with relaxation as we typically did.

With arrangements in place, hotel reservations confirmed for both Sacramento and Honolulu, our bags packed and ready to travel the next day, I sat at the computer excited about our upcoming trip. When the phone rang the voice of a friend who'd helped us find our Hawai'i hotel greeted me saying she guessed our trip was off. What was she talking about? She suggested turning on the TV. Waking Lil with news of this disturbing call we then watched replays of New York's Twin Towers being attacked on September 11, 2001.

Learning all U.S. airports were to be closed for the next few days we discussed driving to Sacramento for the wedding even if we didn't make it to Hawai'i, but realized our bodies simply couldn't take that intense a trip. We resigned ourselves to staying home. Others missed the wedding as well, including the best man. I wouldn't make it to Hawai'i before my 50th birthday.

Two months later, joining my parents for our traditional Thanksgiving holiday, I opened an email from our friend in Hawai'i. He wrote he'd been helping some folks at the University of Hawai'i, in Honolulu, put together a disability studies symposium. Would I be interested in presenting about Disability Culture? Thrilled at the request, I shared the news with everyone we'd go to Hawai'i after all.

Three months later, settling into our airplane seats on the way to Hawai'i, I voiced a premonition to Lil about wanting to live in Hawai'i.

When we arrived and the symposium organizers learned about Lil's own disability rights background, they asked her to work as well. In fact, she ended up doing more than me as she facilitated small group discussions, while I delivered one presentation.

We stayed at a Waikiki Beach hotel, driving to the University each day for the symposium. Whenever possible we'd relax at the hotel beach. Sitting there one day I gazed across the blue ocean, up at the inviting sun, back at the green mountains, and asked myself why didn't we live in Hawai'i?

Contemplating the possibility, we inquired of people we'd just met if they thought there might be a chance we could relocate. We learned how difficult finding housing could be, but a University affiliation might qualify us to live in faculty housing. We didn't have to worry about employment since our SSDI would follow us.

We boarded the plane to leave the island with the promise of new friends assisting us to return if that's what we truly wanted. By the time we landed in El Paso our decision was made. The director of the Center on Disability Studies (CDS), the University of Hawai'i department that sponsored the symposium, appointed both Lil and me as Resident Scholars, making us eligible for faculty housing. We each hoped we'd find some contract work with CDS which we could do while on SSDI. To help pay for the move, I'd also agreed to write a series of essays for an organization I'd often worked with in Texas.

Only one commitment remained on our schedule, conducting a workshop at the Border Book Festival in Las Cruces. After that we'd be free to leave whenever we wished. We began packing.

I wanted one more bone density test before we left New Mexico. Since my terrifying bone density result when applying for the Gaucher Disease protocol led to my starting the Enzyme Replacement Therapy (ERT), annual tests had become part of my routine. No longer immeasurable, the tests always showed severe osteoporosis. I informed the technician that's what she'd find. About halfway through the process she turned to me with a puzzled countenance. "Did you say I'd see severe osteoporosis?" "Yes, that's what I said." Shaking her head, she indicated she observed no sign of osteoporosis. I was stunned. This couldn't have resulted from ERT, which I'd stopped at least six months before. ERT isn't permanent, which is why it's repeated every two weeks. The only explanation for the dramatic change in my bone density, now showing up as average for someone of my age and gender, seemed to come from my ongoing RCT treatments.

Excited about the change in my bones and our upcoming move, we began the process of packing 80 boxes of rocks, and a few other "inconsequential" things, like clothes and a bed, to move with us over the ocean.

Three months after returning from Honolulu we boarded a plane to return there to live. The trip itself wasn't a good omen. In Los Angeles, for our connecting flight, we waited for hours in an ancient terminal for the flight from Hawai'i. The plane had been delayed in Honolulu. By the time it reached LA, we'd sat in the airport longer than our trip to cross the ocean was supposed to take. When we finally arrived in Honolulu, exhausted, hungry, and in pain, we wanted nothing more than the bed in our hotel, where we'd stay for a few days before moving into our new apartment.

While settling into our new home in June of 2002, we also anticipated the 2003 publication of my book, *Movie Stars and Sensuous Scars: Essays on the Journey from Disability Shame to Disability Pride*, which consisted of personal stories about living with Gaucher Disease; pain and disability; and articles about disability rights and culture.

While I completed *Movie Stars*, Herwig also worked on a 2003 book about RCT. He and Alice visited us later that year, bringing copies of *Reconnective Therapy: A New Healing Paradigm*. I read Herwig's words with deliberation, focusing on both the content and how learning more about the work might help me understand my ongoing treatments.

Each day I'd fold aspects of what I learned while reading passages from Herwig's book into my daily meditations. I now also included conscious breathing exercises, inhaling thoughts of love and healing while exhaling ones of fear and pain.

Certain principles in Herwig's book stimulated my own

thinking and imagining. Herwig wrote each of our beliefs and feelings created experiences. Interpreting this statement to mean each of our thoughts might potentially spin off into its own world I conceptualized this idea literally, visualizing multiple "Steve universes" emanating from my thoughts. One specific picture recurred--a universe where "Steve" became the athlete I'd once dreamed of being, before the severity of my disability became apparent. Concentrating on that Steve and his life, he enjoyed a mobile and pain-free life. I usually pictured him running.

I, on the other hand, the Steve in this universe, still lived with chronic, sometimes excruciating pain requiring use of my wheelchair most of the time, and ingestion of a morphine derivative narcotic throughout the day. In our new apartment, negotiating my large, motorized wheelchair in our kitchen was especially difficult. The extension of the chair's leg rest, a platform on which both my feet rested, made it difficult to maneuver in this small space, filled with cupboards and appliances. Only when my pain made walking totally unrealistic did I use my chair in our kitchen.

One such morning, when my pain led to this kind of immobility, I arose and dressed in my uniform of T-shirt and shorts, and entered the kitchen to make a pot of coffee. When the coffee finished brewing, I poured myself a mug, then, in the process of moving my chair in the tiny space, knocked it onto my naked leg. Screaming with pain, the scalding coffee reddening my skin, Lil awoke and nicely offered to clean up the mess. I began to pour cold water on the huge mark forming on my leg, then stopped. Having immersed myself in Herwig's book for weeks I thought I now knew how to use

RCT to heal the burn.

Lying on the bed, I called Herwig, but only reached his voice mail. Leaving a message for him to call me as soon as he could, I then spent the next 15 minutes or so working on repairing my injury. To do this I connected to my own energy body. Then I imagined my leg healing. Within thirty minutes my skin color returned to normal and all signs of damage disappeared. If Lil hadn't seen my leg blistering, she wouldn't have believed I'd ever been burned. But she had and we were both amazed.

Shortly after the redness vanished Herwig called. I described to him what happened and what I'd done. He set down the phone to take a look, then laughing as he picked up the phone again, he remarked while I'd healed the skin, I hadn't worked on the shock to my body, which still lingered, so he'd done that part.

Some months later a similar but less serious burn occurred after carelessly removing a dish from the microwave and feeling steaming juice spilling onto my finger. Maybe it wasn't the kitchen causing my problems? This time working only on the shock, rather than the skin, my finger showed no signs of burn within 10 minutes. Lil witnessed this one, too.

It's one thing to read about RCT, and to experience abstract healing, or even to be the recipient of a treatment, as when I'd injured my hip on the road to Tucson. It's quite another to watch as burns heal before one's eyes. These two experiences erased any remaining doubts I harbored about RCT's potential.

I began to ask Herwig if now he thought being an RCT practitioner would be possible for me. He believed RCT to be a skill anyone could acquire so, yes, he did think that. Not only that but he thought I'd actually been practicing RCT as I'd been working on myself.

One day, during Herwig's ongoing treatments of me, he observed the initiation process. Connections that could be made after initiation facilitated a change in my RCT abilities. I could now access different aspects of the energy world with which I wanted to work.

Many energetic frequencies exist, some of which we encounter on a daily basis, for example when we turn on a light, or watch TV. Other energetic frequencies we might tap into include tuning into another person's thoughts. For instance, many of us have experienced thinking of someone and soon after we receive a call from that individual. When RCT is practiced, connections are made to energetic frequencies on what might be termed a "healing plane." More than one "healing plane" exists. The level and experience of an RCT practitioner will dictate with which "healing plane" someone connects.

Each day, my meditations still filled with projections of myself into another "thought world," where a healthy and running Steve, the active athlete, seemed to feel no pain.

During this process, visions of walking began to form and strengthen daily. This "sight" became so persuasive that one night I turned to Lil and told her I was going for a walk. While she stared at me, wondering what I was talking about, I got up, leaving my wheelchair behind, and headed to the front door. Speechless, she watched me go.

A sidewalk runs in front of four ground floor apartments in our building. Our apartment is at one end. My first walk consisted of going from our front door to the end of the sidewalk in front of the furthest apartment from us and back, a total of a couple hundred yards.

Returning moments later, Lil wanted to know "what exactly was going on?" Explaining how I kept seeing visions of myself walking, and feeling I needed to give it a shot, that's what I did. Astounded, she wondered if I had any notion how bizarre I sounded. I did indeed know how weird this appeared but I had to continue.

I began taking regular walks, without any mobility aids, around our apartment. At first, they remained extremely short. For about a week I walked from our apartment to the other end of our building and back. Feeling no ill effects, my range gradually lengthened. Eventually I walked by all the buildings in the entire multi-building complex. Then I risked walking outside the complex. Then I chanced the uneven gait of crossing a grassy hill. Each night I'd walk farther. I used my wheelchair when I traveled to campus or got in our new van to go anywhere, but I walked around our apartment most of the time.

On my 52nd birthday, Sunday, October 26, 2003, I determined to cross the street and walk to the busy marketplace, about a quarter to a half-mile away. Breathing deeply with each step, concentrating on putting one foot in front of the other without stumbling, and avoiding cracks in the sidewalk, I walked into a small restaurant. No one paid me much mind; I was no more than another customer. Finishing my sandwich, I returned home, excitement building with each footfall.

After I told Lil what I'd just done she was flabbergasted. I hadn't walked that far in years. The next day began treks around our neighborhood, expanding the distance each time. I bought a pedometer. I covered about a mile-and-a-half the day I walked the long way around to the marketplace.

Walking exerted a pull on my psyche unimaginable only weeks before. After not leaving the island in the year-and-a-half since we moved I made plans to visit my parents for Thanksgiving. I decided to go without my wheelchair. Only a month before, I'd walked to the marketplace for the first time. What the heck was I doing?

I'd started using a motorized wheelchair in the first place in large part because of the difficulty of traversing airports. My shoulders and hands ached from pushing a manual wheelchair across terminals and trying to move from one flight to another in a timely fashion. Now I'd chosen to leave my chair behind. Didn't I want to at least take my manual chair for back-up in case something went wrong? No. Everyone thought I was nuts. But my intuition was strong. I needed to do this.

To make this trip more complicated, my sister would meet me in Phoenix and we'd drive to Tucson. My flight would arrive earlier than hers and I'd need to go to another terminal to meet her. Didn't I want to arrange for a chair in the airport to move from one terminal to the next? No. Didn't I want my parents to rent a chair in case I needed it? No.

What if something happened? I didn't have an answer. I just

knew my internal compass mandated I make this trip without my chair. I needed to test my ability to leave my wheelchair behind without any kind of security net.

This trip represented a crossroads. My life had changed. I still had pain. I still perceived myself as a wheelchair user. But somehow, resolving to travel without my chair, I made sure that's what happened. The trip went smoothly, without a hitch. I carried my bags without assistance. I walked onto a bus taking passengers from one terminal to another. At my parents' house we walked around the neighborhood each day. And it all felt good!

My parents, and others who saw me, wanted to know what caused this dramatic transformation? I tried explaining, but it wasn't easy.

How does one offer an explanation of energy? This wasn't like taking a pill or having surgery. Energy work occurs within and is a hard concept for many to grasp. How does one describe an expanding consciousness? I'd brought copies of Herwig's book and shared the concept of an energy body. My sister and Dad took it in. My Mom didn't understand.

But, believing or otherwise, no one could deny the fact of my walking around without my chair. No matter what one could, or could not, integrate into a belief system, I moved for the first time in decades without my chair.

A few months later I traveled to Washington, DC, again without my chair. I had some skepticism about how I'd handle the cold, in the middle of winter, but once again the trip proved doable.

A change occurred after returning home from this trip. My

left ankle wouldn't hold my weight. My doctor thought it resulted from a lack of circulation from spending too much time sitting on the plane. Whatever the cause, the pain lasted for a few weeks. I used my chair while recovering, and then after recuperating my nightly walking routine began once more. I began to use my wheelchair only when I went outside for meetings or classes or other excursions.

In early 2004 I moved from doing contract work at CDS to becoming a part-time employee. Two forces drove this change. First, when we moved to Hawai'i our New Mexico health insurance didn't follow us and we relied solely on Medicare. Medicare didn't reimburse prescription drug costs, and our numerous medications accumulated into thousands of dollars per month. We had to use credit cards to obtain them. Becoming a part-time employee at the University of Hawai'i qualified me for health insurance benefits covering most of our prescription costs. That became my biggest impetus to returning to employment. Secondarily, and making the first choice possible, I sensed I had the energy to work outside the home again.

Chapter 18:

Transformations

Life is like a voyaging canoe. Sometimes when voyaging, we do not see land for great distances and we can lose our sense of direction. The Ancients knew that even on a clear night when all stars are available, there was one star that can guide you best. Like the ancients we must also find that one true star—our connection to Spirit—and the place to search is in the depths of your soul.

Kaniela Akaka

The day my internal voice guided me toward a set of steps I thought I'd lost my mind. I'd steered clear of steps of any kind for as long as I could recall. Like any other wheelchair user, steps were the bane of my existence. They prevented me from getting where I wanted to go. I didn't like stairs any better when I emerged from my wheelchair and began walking. The physical act of walking up, and especially down, stairs had always been one of my most painful experiences. It stressed my joints and bones so much I always went out of my way to travel a smooth, or ramped, path into a building.

When I realized one day my body kept pushing me toward a set of stairs I resisted. This particular entryway, to a building I often entered, had ramped access as well, so why take the steps? But my body persisted in moving me toward them. Unable to ignore this strong internal message, I started to take these stairs several times over the next few weeks. Befuddled but following my intuition, I still couldn't imagine why I was drawn to these steps.

Shortly thereafter the Center on Disability Studies, where I'd now become a full-time Assistant Professor, hosted our annual spring conference, which attracts about a thousand participants. As usual, I sat in my chair in the midst of the large crowd where people milled about, but I also found myself getting out of my chair and walking around quite a bit. At one point, I left my wheelchair in another room and moved on my own through the conference.

I paid attention to how much I walked at this conference and to my recent mysterious attraction to stairs, without knowing how to integrate these experiences. A week after the conference ended came another radical change.

One morning I plopped in my wheelchair ready to leave home for a meeting, but when I flipped the power switch to "on" nothing happened. The chair clearly had a malfunction. I thought for a minute or two, then decided to walk to the bus stop about half a mile away and get on a bus, rather than cancel my participation in the meeting.

I'd traveled by bus before. But I'd always used my wheelchair, made easy because Honolulu has one of the most extensive, accessible bus systems in the country. I'd never walked onto a bus. When the bus arrived I climbed the steps and sat down. At my destination I got off the same way. Then it hit me. I'd been using stairs to prepare myself for this day; the day I'd have to ride the bus.

After I returned home, riding the bus once more, I got my

chair repaired. But I decided my chair not working had been a sign. I paid attention and stopped using it. A few months later we placed the chair in our storage closet.

My process of transforming from regular wheelchair use to walking revealed to me two ways to react to twinges of bone pain. Since Gaucher Disease (GD) first manifested itself, and especially after my bones began breaking as a teenager, the onset of bone pain meant treading carefully, taking care not to push myself or the likely result would be a fracture. A different way of viewing that same twinge could be to focus on healing--rather than expecting a bone to break--perhaps connecting my body with healing energy.

These two attitudes paralleled my attitude about moving from using a wheelchair to walking full-time. Deciding one day to walk and then doing it did not come easily. How might walking affect my life? What would happen to my relationship with Lil? The way we experienced disability had been one of our basic connections. Understanding the experiences of wheelchair use and sharing pain, fatigue, and limited energy on a daily basis had been instrumental to our initial compatibility.

When walking began to become a reality for me we dissected the change. Lil worried my conversion might push me to leave her. Trying to reassure her more existed to our relationship than our mutual wheelchair use, we discussed ways to release this fear, with the primary one acknowledging it wasn't what either one of us wanted.

Another concern reared itself over work. For twenty years, living and breathing disability rights as someone with a visible, disabling condition had been advantageous. When entering a room using a wheelchair no one questions whether you have the requisite experience to make a case for promoting disability rights. That's not always true with people whose disabilities aren't apparent or who have no disability at all. Having been guilty of making these assumptions myself, I understood this reality. At the same time, having lived with disability for almost fifty years, whatever might happen in the future couldn't alter my knowledge or experiences. Most importantly, my passion for the movement and its goals remained.

Thinking about Lil and work and disability one thought recurred: whatever else might happen my path, my destiny, must be pursued. Choosing otherwise--not being true to myself-- most likely would lead to some kind of breakdown, physically, mentally, emotionally, or all three. If maintaining my integrity meant walking and walking might change my life, that's what would have to happen.

Herwig invited me to a Reconnective Therapy practitioner training in Santa Fe in December of 2004. We discussed several times how to make this happen in the middle of winter. Where I'd stay became my greatest fear. Sleeping at Herwig and Alice's house would lessen expenses and be more convenient, but the only available room would be cold and drafty. I decided to stay at a nearby hotel. Logistics unraveled, I boarded a plane to travel to Santa Fe.

Five of us participated, four from out-of-state, including one who traveled from Germany for the week-long session. The primary method of training was performing RCT itself, with Herwig's guidance. Before arriving in Santa Fe, we'd all been asked to schedule five people willing to have us work on them. Herwig also integrated

our practice time into a regular treatment group. Since each partici-
pant also treated people located in many geographic regions, we had
chances to practice RCT both in person and long distance, or re-
motely, via phone calls.

After solving the issue of where to stay, my biggest concern
going into the week was the final day of training when we were
scheduled to work with horses. Although I couldn't recall the last
time I'd been around horses, my overall trepidation stemmed less
from my lack of familiarity with these animals than knowing we'd
be required to stand for several hours. Herwig assured me if the need
to sit arose he'd take care of it.

On the last day we traveled to a stable. On our way there we
stopped to work with several other horses. Standing next to a horse
amplified their magnificence--and their size. They're huge. The
horses sensed my discomfort in their shadow. At the stable, aware of
my unease, Herwig suggested working with three or four horses
without touching them, as some of my classmates did. Remaining on
my feet for several hours didn't become a problem because it didn't
cause any pain.

Excited about every aspect of the RCT training experience
and my new status as a practitioner trainee, I boarded a plane for
home. There, the most shocking change so far occurred.

While walking represented a huge change, my hidden disability of chronic pain had always impacted my life more than my
mobility impairment. I'd lived with pain much longer than with not
being ambulatory. That too changed.

This only dawned when I realized my intake of narcotics had

slowed. Paying attention to my lessening pain and wanting to see if the need for pain medication still existed, I stopped taking it.

I'd always gone cold turkey when I wanted to get off a medication, but this time it didn't work. Not because of my pain, which had essentially disappeared, but because sleep now eluded me. After a week of mostly sleepless nights I started taking my pain medication so I could sleep. But since my body no longer needed it, except to sleep, I kept taking it later and later during the day. I still planned to get off it. Discussing this with Herwig, he thought RCT could help the process, but suggested waiting until I had a few leisurely days to withdraw.

When that time finally arrived I'd also spoken with my doctor about getting off the pain medications. He prescribed two drugs, one to assist with sleep and another to alleviate withdrawal symptoms. Within a few days I stopped taking both these drugs and all my pain medication for the first time since first being diagnosed with GD. I don't describe myself as pain free, but I no longer have chronic pain and I don't believe my pain is much different than other people about my age who've had similar life experiences.

Suddenly, in my 50s, after decades of paralyzing pain and immobility, neither were the center of my life. I walked to my new car, which didn't have hand controls, to go to work or anywhere else. Boarding a plane nobody paid attention to me. My anonymity thrilled me.

Someone meeting me for the first time might wonder why my right knee angled away from my body or why I slumped a bit in a chair, but they wouldn't know those characteristics resulted from years of broken bones.

Did I still have a disability? I don't lift weights that are too heavy. I get tired and fatigued. I still don't run. If Lil and I are outside in a driving rain, she can zoom ahead of me in her motorized wheelchair. I don't have as much energy as many of my co-workers—but neither do many other people. I don't have a pat answer to the question of whether my changes have made me nondisabled. Perhaps that's because of the word "disability" itself.

Over the years numerous attempts to come up with a better word have occurred, but none have succeeded. Maybe that's because whether someone has a disability isn't the crucial issue—it's how someone is treated because of disability. From that standpoint, discrimination and oppression continue to be a significant national—and worldwide—problem. All the issues related to disability raised in this book remain and therefore I still proudly belong to the disability rights movement.

At the same time, perceptions of myself and my potential contributions to this movement evolved. How might what I've learned in this journey away from pain and immobility be applied to the movement?

The greatest lesson learned in this process has been the ability to alter conceptions of reality. My physical changes didn't result from willpower; instead, these transformations happened after my views of the world changed. Feeling twinges in my bones and focusing on healing rather than pain is a perfect example of my internal revolution. Looking at the world differently may have been my key to moving beyond physical pain.

At first, I didn't know what caused my pain to stop. I assumed the continued impact of my ongoing RCT treatments, both from Herwig and my own internal work played a role in lessening my pain. But during this time Lil had trouble getting her pain medications filled. Frustrated and angry, we listened to our physician explain insurance companies controlled how often someone could obtain medicine.

While this appointment dealt with Lil's medications, I wondered how long I could depend on insurance companies for my own medication? Looking back at when my chronic pain disappeared, getting so angry at the power of the insurance company and not wanting to depend on this unfeeling bureaucracy may have led me to create a new reality in which my anger became transformed into expelling my chronic pain.

Since all of these changes happened, I've returned to using my chair only once. This resulted from an inexplicable episode. At a meeting one day, in the late autumn of 2006, I felt perfectly comfortable until I stood up and a pain in my left leg like a cramp or a Charley horse stopped me. Expecting the pain to go away, I boarded a flight later that day for a conference in Washington, DC. When the meetings ended, another flight took me to Tucson to visit my folks. But the pain never dissipated. Instead it moved up my leg to my hip. Worsening as the trip continued, I still walked, though my pace slowed with each day. By the time I traveled home and got off the plane in Honolulu and into our van when Lil picked me up, it seemed my body, knowing I'd made it safely home, announced "okay, enough."

At our apartment, getting from the van to the bed became excruciating. Unable to move at all without great pain, Lil retrieved my chair from the storage closet. I used it for about a week, then the pain diminished and I began walking again. That's the last time I used my chair.

This experience also became the first test of not using narcotics to deal with pain. Not wanting to go back to them, I used over-the-counter drugs, like aspirin, but avoided prescription pain medications. Asking Herwig what in the world was going he recommended being calm and waiting it out as my bones were "simply" changing and the process caused my pain. Comparing this situation to when I lay on my Norman bed, back broken and immersed in pain, focused almost exclusively on when I could next swallow narcotics to try and lessen how much I hurt, the road traveled to this point in my life could not have been more surprising.

Part III: Liberation

If knowledge is power then understanding is liberation.

Manulani Aluli-Meyer

Chapter 19:

Forgetting the What, Remembering the Who

Your task is enormous:
Your task is light as a feather.

A lifelong battle stalks me. There is so much to do and so little time. Remembering to breathe is sometimes a chore. Rest isn't an option. Work compels me.

It's Saturday morning and in front of the computer I sit eager to complete this book. I will do the same tomorrow and every weekend day until finishing. My own internal pressures are multiplied by an external deadline. Sections of the manuscript need to be shared within weeks with a sponsor of a speaking engagement. But it's not ready—I'm not ready. On weekends a rapid transition is required from my daily work into this manuscript. Relaxation must wait. Breaks are an unaffordable luxury.

Digging deep into my own psyche and churning the past into words, both for my own enlightenment and hopefully to positively impact others, takes a toll. My body rebels. My knee hurts more than it has in years, but I can't stop. The work must go on. Breaks are self-indulgent. Why do I have so much drive?

A few years ago, working with a healer to relieve a lifetime of stresses, we returned to the womb. When commenting about how my mother's womb must have provided great security and love because my birth occurred two weeks late, an observation I'd made many times before, she disagreed. Remaining in the womb she believed had more to do with the life tasks I'd set for myself. They were many and large and knowing this I hesitated to get started—to be born.

Imagine someone telling you that your life's purpose—your reason for being on the planet--is to heal a species. Although this is not what she said—the actual content is private—it's close enough. I sat stunned, wondering why anyone would aspire to such a lofty objective and how it might be accomplished? But, before this information could be processed, the healer unveiled several other goals, all similar in magnitude. Breathing deeply and storing her observations for future use, we moved on to other topics. But the revelations didn't disappear. When we returned to them a year later they hadn't changed. What are the possibilities of finishing all these tasks?

Feeling pressure during the week to complete the requirements of my job--a to-do list itself capable of consuming each waking hour--so I can focus during the weekend on this manuscript, and errands, and connecting with family and friends—generates an endless to-do list. The number of hours devoted each day to accomplishments expand. My wife worries. She reminds me nothing will get done if I forget to take care of myself and I'm no longer here. Hearing her words doesn't stop me.

In the midst of my frenzy to do all these tasks my knee began to hurt. Knowing healing is part of what I now do, of who I am, I'm confident the pain will dissipate within a few days. But it doesn't and for the first time in years I find myself limping around our apartment. I retrieve my cane. Why isn't healing occurring? Contacting Herwig he responds my knee is undergoing energetic shifts and the pain is part of the healing process. But perhaps something else is at play as well—a life lesson. Caught up in my whirlwind of doing, refusing to acknowledge a need to relax, my body takes control.

The pain in my knee slowed me down, enforcing limitations on what could be accomplished in a day. Lying on the bed, using the space to meditate on these circumstances, a phrase started penetrating my awareness: forget the what, remember the who. What did this mean?

Reflecting further raised the question if all these tasks really matter? What happens if I leave the planet without finishing everything I want and believe I need to accomplish? That answer is fairly simple: either they won't get done or someone else will do them. We all have only so many hours—in a day, a week, or a lifetime. We can fill them with tasks, my tendency—or we can use them in other ways.

What happens when ambitions--the "what," or in my case, the work, overwhelms the person I'm striving to become—the "who"? When becoming so focused on attainment leads me down the path of forgetting to relax and enjoy life, to find the humor in myself and in everyday situations, to connect with those who love me and who I love, when the "what" overwhelms the "who".

What does the work matter if I lose myself in the process? How can peace be made from this internal war? Recalling the major epiphany of my life—lying in a hospital bed and choosing not to be a victim fills my consciousness. Overwhelmed by the work before me an attitude of helplessness, of victimization, prevails—there's so much to do, there's not enough time to do anything else. This feeling of persecution is a recurring theme of my life. Resolving it is simple—which doesn't mean it's easy. Just as with Gaucher Disease, all these ambitions, goals—the work, the "what"-- are neutral. It's up to me to choose to be, or not to be, a victim.

Whether breaks, relaxation, and rejuvenation are necessary is less important than my understanding, my remembering to decide to enjoy what I'm doing—to derive pleasure from my life's tasks, from both the "what" and the "who" of my life. Martyrdom, not the actual loss of life for a cause, but wallowing in suffering, choosing to draw attention to myself—internally, externally, or both—as a victim unable to extract myself from this role does more to separate me from my life's tasks than almost anything else I can conceive because victimization is a means of separation.

My desire, whether it's as a teacher, writer, healer, husband, father, grandfather, or any other role, is connection. When forgetting this truth my life lesson of "forgetting the what and remembering the who" will constantly recur until I pay attention.

While this book is my story, the patterns described in it— pain, anger, accomplishment, isolation, victimization, disease, connection, healing, and others—aren't unique to me. Mining my personal experiences is one way to channel and explore universal truths. But fascination with an individual life and becoming mired in its details is when we're most likely to neglect our connections to others, to forget to reach beyond ourselves.

Some thoughts and methods to move beyond individual experiences and tap into the greater universe are shared next.

Chapter 20:

Practical Applications

Be still.
Hear your heart.
Feel your soul.
In joy.
With love.

Creativity, whether composing music, creating a meal, or conceiving a child, are godlike achievements connecting humans to eternity, to something permanent outside of ourselves. Each of these activities involves three traits: first, inspiration, or motivation; second, creation, or an opportunity to be imaginative; and third, connection, or a unity beyond ourselves.

We all know people who don't like to cook when they're alone. They see no point in expending their energy on such a solitary endeavor. They want, indeed they need, their efforts to be rewarded with connection. This involves a spiritual link because the creator of the meal seeks connection beyond their individual personality, their own unique experience.

Few of us are satisfied with physical well-being unless we also feel spiritually healthy. Spiritual attainment comes in many forms. Like pain, it's unique to each individual. Forcing one kind of spirituality on someone else is doomed to failure because we all have diverse needs, but when we find a spiritual path that resonates with us, feels comfortable to us, enhances our well being, our health, then many of us seek like-minded individuals.

We may find spiritual peers in typical places of worship, such as churches, synagogues, and mosques. We may also find them in nature, espousing a cause or pursuing a passion. It doesn't really matter where or how we find our spiritual cohort. What's imperative is we do locate them. We need this spiritual connectedness as much as we need the physical kind.

Few of us wish to be without human companionship. Maybe no one wishes to be alone, if one adds nature into that mixture. At some level we all want to be loved and to love.

I recall Herwig's describing *A Course in Miracles*, as "there is nothing in the universe, except love." That's a statement I need to recall when stuck in my pain, my work, or myself. The link between us all is love. It's not in the content of accomplishment but in the love that sparks it. In the *Course* itself the illusion of fear is depicted as the opposite of love. Fear is an illusion because it's unreal—a choice made when we forget love. In the midst of my life fear takes over when the entanglements of everyday life engulf me to such a great extent my attention becomes limited to details and I lose sight of the meaning behind them.

Disruptions of all sorts drag me from my center—from my connection with something greater than myself. The most difficult part for me in remaining healthy, or whole, is avoiding distraction, or recognizing which distractions need my attention. Being interrupted, for instance, while writing frazzles me, yet composition of the initial draft of this book occurred in the living room of our apartment in the middle of all kinds of chaos. Few disturbances were major, and another person wouldn't find them annoying. But I did.

In the preceding paragraph, I deliberately chose the word "chaos" to emphasize how so many things can upset my sense of order. But is it reasonable, or even fair, to blame something outside myself for being pulled away from my center?

A major distraction might be hearing a crash, rushing into the next room and discovering Lil fell and may be hurt. This has far more significance than being interrupted while writing, but both the noise of the crash and the possibility of injury may pull me away from my center. At the same time, both are also capable of leading me back to my center. In each case, the event is not the distraction; my reaction to it is. I can choose not to fall into the victim role and look at the situation as presenting an opportunity to provide love to someone who needs it. Knowing this and acting from it, especially in the moment of commotion, are two different things.

Such distractions, no matter their origin or import, invade the space many of us carve for ourselves. Enclaves of solitude, like monasteries and convents, are created in part to eliminate diversions. With fewer disturbances we're more likely to find our center and connect to our version of God, or something beyond ourselves. Most of us, however, don't have the luxury or desire to be secluded from the world. Some religious traditions even advocate being within the world as the only way we can truly be integrated, because being able to center ourselves within the chaos that is everyday life is a real test of faith. When we achieve tranquility in the midst of confusion we may construct something outside of ourselves.

At least once a day I become centered by meditating. When starting this practice I meditated in the afternoons. Since returning to fulltime work my daily timeframe changed and I now choose to begin each day with meditation, to prepare and excite myself for the day ahead. Each morning gratitude fills much of my meditation, thanking, in various ways, my spiritual guides for supporting me. That's when remembering who I am is most easily conveyed to my own consciousness.

Being centered is key. Without being able to move into quiet spaces, contemplative places, I'm distracted by the constant hum of routine. When we're able to locate our center we give ourselves opportunity to connect with our higher selves, our essence, or whatever other term feels applicable.

How can we do this? For many of us finding our own center, our core, presents more difficulties than physically connecting with another person. Western cultures, in particular, teach us from an early age to believe only what we perceive with our own eyes. There are hundreds if not thousands or more examples of how this instruction is not only inaccurate but a disservice.

Electricity is a perfect example. If you stopped someone on the street and asked them to describe what electricity looked like, chances are they'd flounder, but if you asked them if they believed in the power of electricity to, for instance, turn on a light, power a refrigerator, or keep an oven operational, they'd probably have no trouble agreeing it works.

We cannot see electricity with our physical vision, but we know it works. If our homes contained only appliances whose power we could see, we'd no longer have computers, televisions, radios, air conditioning, and many other items taken for granted.

Western cultures emphasize five senses: hearing, touch, sight, smell, and taste. But we all have many more senses, including temperature, pain, balance, and spatial and time awareness. Intuitiveness is another phenomenon, perhaps a sense, we ascribe to ourselves and others. Many of us lose our sense of intuition in our younger years because Western cultural norms tend to invalidate these feelings.

We are often told to grow up and be logical when we persist in attending to our feelings, rather than what is perceived to be rational. For many of us, a tension exists between what our gut, or intuition, tells us and what can be seen with our own eyes. But at some level we all realize aspects of life exist outside of our limited physical senses. For some of us this awareness is so scary, so intimidating, we repudiate it. This denial sometimes makes connecting outside of ourselves difficult. To achieve a spiritual connection, however, we have to figure out how to go beyond the limitations of our body.

Observing someone die reinforces the finiteness of our physicality. I watched my father pass on in the summer of 2007. I touched him both moments before and after he died. His body looked identical, but it didn't feel the same. Before death he was warm; afterward he was cold. Clearly no longer my father, his body looked no different. What changed? His spirit passed from his body. Someone else might choose other words, but whatever animated him no longer existed within his body. One second it was there, the next it was not.

I could still see my father's body lying before me, but I didn't see my father. He'd moved elsewhere, or ceased to exist at all, depending on one's belief system. My belief system tells me he passed on, that is, the energy that activated his body moved on to somewhere else in the universe.

How do we move beyond our five senses to connect with something greater than ourselves? How do we become so still-- mentally, emotionally, and physically, letting go of our external and internal dramas and traumas--we might find it possible to connect to something greater than ourselves?

Before uniting with something larger than our own physical presence, we must begin by letting go of whatever values and pre-conceptions we already hold. It's a great deal easier to surrender a cherished keepsake than a deeply held belief. Sometimes we're not even aware of convictions we harbor until they're wrenched from us.

Whether these values are perceived as positive or negative is immaterial. The important feat is being able to let go. When we find ourselves capable of releasing our grip on some article of faith the result is we move toward centering ourselves in neutrality.

This kind of impartiality is not apathy; instead it's a form of detachment from our own judgments and prejudices. If we can locate ourselves in a space of neutrality, if only for a few seconds, which is all most of us can tolerate at the beginning of this journey, we com-municate our desire to liberate ourselves from our own biases to a force, or energy, outside of ourselves.

When we live as much as we can from our essence, or our soul or spirit, we move through the universe at higher frequencies than when we live from our ego. This eases our ability to connect to the universe outside ourselves. We all routinely tap into various frequencies, or wavelengths. I type this book on a computer producing a certain energy and listen to music producing another energetic frequency. Nearby, two different kinds of lights provide two additional frequencies. On the table next to me a cordless phone imparts another frequency, and when it rings another emission, and at least one more frequency is supplied by a person at the other end of the line.

I frequently work with a fan blowing in my direction, producing yet another frequency. While I'm in one room, Lil may turn on the television in another, adding yet another frequency. On the TV are actors, salespeople, animals, and animations, all of which carry their own frequencies. A car alarm just blared, adding still one more frequency.

We are constantly surrounded by frequencies of one sort or another. But we also emanate our own frequencies, or energies, into this mix. Have you ever been sitting in a roomful of people at a party, either quietly enjoying yourself or engaged in animated conversation, when a stranger enters the room and everything stops for a moment? That newcomer stamped their energy onto the party merely by being present. Conversely, in the same situation another person might arrive and no one notices? Each of those individuals brings their unique energy into the party. One discharges such a strong frequency every other person in the room stops what they're doing to pay attention. The other person gives off such mild energy no one pays any mind.

Those of us unable to maintain life at these higher frequencies tend to be drawn by our personalities into the mundane. At the personality level, we are energetically moving at lower frequencies than when we are connected via our essence with the expansive universe.

We all know, or have heard, of people who live at higher frequencies more of the time than the rest of us. They tend to be more focused, more present, and "luckier," while living in the "now" than many of the rest of us. The most skilled we often recognize as wise teachers like the Dalai Lama.

Each of us transmits our own energy signature, as distinctive as a fingerprint. I know several individuals who will do all they possibly can to avoid a crowd. Others will do all they can to be immersed in one. They are attracted or repelled for the same reason— the intense energy whipped up in a throng. The energy released by one person is not only multiplied, but intensified and magnified when melded with others. In my experience, demonstrating at Southern Illinois University, sensations of righteousness while sitting with my friends coexisted with indignation at those who sat on the railroad tracks.

Energy signatures enable Reconnective Therapy to succeed. When an RCT practitioner is at work, our first task is to center our own energy. This frequently means being aware of how widespread we've allowed our own energy to become. This may sound farfetched. An example of how one's energy may enlarge hit home with me on an airplane ride.

Anyone who travels these days knows how narrow airline seats have become. The space between rows also seems to have diminished. Anyone with long or sensitive legs is in danger of having the person sitting in front of us push their seat all the way back and into our own space—or body. On one such ride I got the idea I could push my energy into the space of the person in front of me, who'd moved his seat all the way back and who clearly didn't care what inconvenience he caused. Concentrating for a moment on moving my energy into his space resulted within five minutes of him pulling his seat all the way up, and there it stayed for the duration of the flight.

While extremely pleased with myself, I no longer manifest my energy in this way. It felt wrong to enter someone else's energetic space without their permission. This is assault rather than access. This is also why we always seek permission before working on someone.

Because we may not be aware of our energy expansion, an exercise RCT practitioners are taught when we first begin to work on others is to bring our own energy all the way within our own bodies, then release it to become even with our skin. Leveling our energy in this fashion assists us to work in concert with another person without invading their energy.

RCT work itself occurs at higher frequencies than our typical daily ones. This is why practitioners usually enter a meditative state. When we connect with our own higher frequencies, or energies, we're able to detect another person's energetic signature. We're then able to tap into the frequencies of the energetic body, which is where RCT work, re-connecting aspects of the energetic and physical bodies, or healing, is accomplished.

The details of how RCT works are explained in depth in Herwig Schoen's book so I won't repeat them here (see the Reference on p. 216 for finding his book). What's important to know in the context of this chapter is a straightforward practical application: RCT's effectiveness results from love. The love a practitioner expresses in connecting with the person they work with and the love that fills the universe with which a practitioner connects. Remaining in this space of love is too difficult for most of us to maintain most of the time. If we could we'd no longer need to be here. But the love we bring to our practice, to our lives, makes it possible to facilitate the connections between the energy and physical bodies that have so positively changed my life.

I began this story with a descent into pain, chronic, intense, and acute, leading me on a path of isolation and anger. In the midst of that angst, changing the world became my goal and learning how to foment a successful revolution led me to the study of history. Ready to pursue the life of a scholar, instead discrimination because of my disability steered me on another path. Finding the disability rights movement created a kind of meaning and joy that had been absent from my life until connecting with others who experienced similar life stories.

My desire to provoke change, to make the world a better place, a conscious choice in early adulthood, evolved in middle age into a profound internal revolution. The practice of RCT led to a reversal of seemingly unalterable conditions of pain and immobility.

Could there be a more practical application?

Top: Steve: 5 months
Lower left: Steve and Marda Brown, June 1953
Lower right: Steve, January 1954

Steve at home in Norman, OK in the late 1980s

Steve at the English Gardens in Munich, Germany
in the 1990s

Lillian Gonzales Brown and Steve at a wedding in
Alaska in the 1990s

Steve and Lillian at a wedding at
White Sands, New Mexico

Steve at White Sands, New Mexico

Steve presenting a poster at the Association of University Centers on Disability Conference in Washington, DC, 2008

Epilogue:

The Rest of My Life

Your body is boundless.
It is channeling the energy, creativity,
and intelligence of the entire universe.
Deepak Chopra

Hearing myself, I didn't comprehend the meaning of my response when I told Ulrike, while laying under the PST® machine, that it was time to focus on healing. But from that instant forward movement toward healing filled my life.

The best definition of pain I know is "it hurts." While we all experience pain, each of us has unique, subjective experiences.

What does it mean to hurt? We usually, or at least I, think about physical pain—in my particular case, what does it feel like to experience a broken bone; arthritic joint; bone crisis; sustained, unlocalized chronic pain; or any other kind of bodily ailment? Physical pain can be so intense it interferes with anyone's daily activities; in fact, it can be so invasive it can lead to thoughts of hopelessness, suicide, and murder. It's almost indescribable how impactful serious physical pain may be. Despite this intensity, physical pain often feels more endurable than other kinds of damage.

Physical pain, especially the kind of hurting that results from or leads to disability, has a tendency to segregate the individual living with this kind of pain from others. There are many reasons for such isolation. For example, an individual who lives in constant, intense pain often has difficulty leaving a residence.

Individuals who don't live with chronic pain frequently cannot understand how internally and externally isolating pain can be and how it may lead to an inability, or reluctance, to wander from home. They simply cannot fathom the amount of energy it takes to prepare oneself—first, to get ready to leave home; second, to venture into an often physically, or otherwise, unfriendly environment that's likely to increase someone's pain; third, to understand that since pain is invisible a person's needs may be greeted with disdain; for example, someone who appears healthy may need to ask for help loading groceries into a vehicle; and fourth, to summon the internal fortitude required to be out in the world while in pain and at the same time knowing how much effort it will take to recover from being away from a physically relaxing environment.

When we're out in the world, especially if indications of our pain are evident, those people we're around may fear we're contagious, or defective, and not want either themselves or their loved ones to be around us. Even in immense pain, individuals are usually able to sense when someone doesn't want us around. Whether this results from fear or for some other reason is immaterial. Socially ingrained negative attitudes about disability tend to leave distaste in our wake. We know, both intuitively and objectively, how intensely people just plain don't want to associate with us, be associated with us--or be us.

Health, healing, or wellness is often unattainable if someone feels isolated or disconnected. A healthy feeling follows when one senses with all their being they are part of something larger than themselves, whether that be a peer group, society, or some other entity.

It matters not if we are in pain or feeling as healthy as can be. When we are valued, when we contribute to whatever group we wish to be a part of, we experience a connection with others leading us outside of ourselves--the opposite of isolation. From such associations, we offer ourselves, our abilities, our gifts, to someone else, or some group(s). These individuals or group(s) benefit from our involvement, our presence. We not only provide someone else with our own valuable resources but enhance everyone's feelings of community.

When we, any one of us, find our identity traveling from a sense of isolation to community, we feel better about ourselves. We feel healthier. Wellness—health--is often linked to connectedness and connectedness is linked to love. As human beings, we crave alliances. When we bond with one another, almost all of us feel better.

Recently traveling across the country, when arriving at the airport, I boarded the plane along with everyone else. I made sure I had an aisle seat so I could get up once an hour and walk around the plane. When the pilot turned off the seat belt light I wandered to the back to let the blood flow into my legs and feet. While I stood for a few minutes a flight attendant started conversing with me. It turned out she also lived in Honolulu and we began about a 30 minute conversation. While we talked she continued to work, engaged with other passengers who also wandered toward the back to stretch their legs or get a drink, and responded to various requests for her attention.

I contemplated the enormous changes in my life while standing in the back of the speeding jet. My first plane ride at the age of five became a harbinger of years of pain and disability. This journey, standing and connecting with the flight attendant without any reference to immobility or a wheelchair still amazed me. I wondered where my next travels would take me? Wherever it will be, I'll be ready. I returned to my seat for about an hour then got up again and traversed the length of the plane to ensure the blood continued to circulate as best it could within these narrow confines. I continued this pattern across the ocean until the pilot instructed us to prepare for landing. I gazed towards the windows overlooking my island home.

When the plane landed, I walked to the luggage carousel, picked up my bag and then headed for the sidewalk where I waited for Lil to pick me up. When she drove up I hoisted the bags into the back of the van. I walked to the front and climbed in. When we arrived home I carried my suitcases inside.

I stretched my legs. I'd forgotten about the wheelchair stashed in the storage closet. I hadn't swallowed a pain pill in many years. I walked to the bedroom, got onto the bed and made myself comfortable. Maybe the next day I'd walk to the store and pick up some groceries. I didn't give it much thought. Since my pain has quieted I'm eager to walk into the rest of my life.

References

Akaka, Kaniela. Quoted by Michael B. Carino in "Sail On." Re-
    trieved from:
    http://www.photoworkshop.com/bv/viewimage/176932

Bailey, H.C. Quote retrieved from Brainy Quote.
    http://www.brainyquote.com/quotes/quotes/h/hcbailey177
    125.html

Brown, Steven E., *Independent Living: Theory and Practice.* (Las
    Cruces, NM: Institute on Disability Culture, 1994).

Brown, Steven E., *Investigating a Culture of Disability: Final Re-
    port.* (Las Cruces, NM: Institute on Disability Culture,
    1994). Quote on p. 122 from p. 12.

Brown, Steven E., *Journey Home: A Miracles Poetry, Prayer, and
    Meditation Workbook.* (Las Cruces, NM: Sunrise Point Pub-
    lications, 2001). Quote at beginning of Chapter 19 from
    "Distractions," p. 63. Quote at beginning of Chapter 20 from
    "Of the Heart," p. 47.

Brown, Steven E., *Movie Stars and Sensuous Scars: Essays on the
    Journey from Disability Shame to Disability Pride.* (New
    York: iUniverse, 2003). Quotes, Part I and on pp. 33-35 from
    "Hidden Treasure," pp. 18 and 20. Poem on pp. 14-16
    adapted from "A Healing Journey," pp. 182-86. Quote at be-
    ginning of Chapter 10 from "The Walkout," p. 32. Quote at
    beginning of Chapter 11 from "We Are Who We Are...So

Who Are We?" pp. 80-81. Quote on pp. 111 from "Creating a Disability Mythology, p. 72.

Brown, Steven E., *Pain, Plain and Fancy Rappings: Poetry from the Disability Culture.* (Las Cruces, NM: Institute on Disability Culture, 1995). Stanzas on p. 113-14 from "Tell Your Story," p. 7. Quotes on p. 121 from "Pain, Plain," pp. 1, 3.

Brown, Steven E., *Voyages: Life Journeys.* (Las Cruces, NM: Institute on Disability Culture, 1996). "In Need of Comedy," pp. 11-12. Quote from "Sonata in the Lingering Keys of Life," on pp. 137-38 from p. 4-5. Quote from "What Do You Do When Your Dreams Come True?" on p. 139, from p. 33.

Bottomley, Sylvia. Quote from author's personal papers.

Buddha. Thinkexist.com. Retrieved from:
http://thinkexist.com/quotation/holding_on_to_anger_is_l ike_grasping_a_hot_coal/12958.html

Burton, Barbara K. Quote from author's personal papers.

de Chardin, Pierre Teilhard. Goodreads. Retrieved from:
http://www.goodreads.com/author/quotes/5387.Pierre_Te ilhard_de_Chardin

Chopra, Deepak, *Reinventing the Body, Resurrecting the Soul.* (New York: Harmony, 2009). Quote on p. 8.

A Course in Miracles. (New York: Viking, 1975).

Crocker, Allen C. Quote from author's personal papers.

Graham, Robert J. Quote from author's personal papers.

Hayles, S. B. Quotes from author's personal papers.

Keller, Helen. "Famous Quotes and Authors." Retrieved from:
http://www.famousquotesandauthors.com/authors/helen_

keller_quotes.html

King, Martin Luther, Jr. (Aug. 28, 1963). "I Have a Dream." Retrieved from http://www.americanrhetoric.com/speeches/mlkihaveadream.htm

King, Martin Luther, Jr. (April 3, 1968). "I've Been to the Mountaintop." Retrieved from http://www.americanrhetoric.com/speeches/mlkivebeentothemountaintop.htm

McDonald, Joe. (1965). "I-Feel-Like-I'm-Fixin'-To-Die-Rag."

Meyer, Manulani Aluli "Indigenous and Authentic: Native Hawaiian Epistemology and the Triangulation of Meaning," in L. Smith, N. Denzin, & Y. Lincoln, *Handbook of Critical and Indigenous Methodologies*, Ch. 11, pp. 217-33, (Newbury Park, CA: Sage, 2008), quote on p. 229.

Melody, *Love is in the Earth: A Kaleidoscope of Crystals.* (Wheatridge, CO: Earth-Love Publishing, 1995).

de Saint-Exupéry, Antoine, *The Little Prince.* (Paris: Gallimard, 1943).

Saint-Pierre, Gaston, Boater, Debbie, and Shapiro, Debbie (1991). *The Metamorphic Technique: Principles and Practice.* (New York: Lillian Barber).

Schoen, Herwig, *Reconnective Therapy: A New Healing Paradigm.* (Santa Fe, NM: RCT Publishing, 2003). Quote at beginning of Chapter 15 from Reconnective Therapy: A New Healing Paradigm website: http://www.reconnectivetherapy.com/

Sloan, Howard R. Quote from author's personal papers.

Soifer, Aviam, "Disabling the ADA: Essences, Better Angels, and Unprincipled Neutrality Claims," *William and Mary Law Review*, 44 (3), (February 2003), pp.1285-1340.

Williams, G. Rainey and Dakil, S. E. Quote from author's personal papers.

Institute on Disability Culture

The Institute on Disability Culture is a tax-exempt, 501(c)(3) not-for-profit organization. Our mission is: Promoting pride in the history, activities and cultural identity of people with disabilities throughout the world. We do this with training, consultation, presentation, research, and publications throughout the U.S. and other countries. Check us out at:

http://www.instituteondisabilityculture.org

Reconnective Therapy-Hawai'i

For more information on Steve's RCT work, check out:

http://www.reconnectivetherapyhawaii.org